My road to Indy

A Narrative by Len Sutton

Cover photos
left, descending:
Len Sutton in his first race, 1946 (*photo courtesy of Pete Sukalac*);
Len's last competitive year at the Indianapolis Motor Speedway, 1965 (*photo courtesy of the Indianapolis Motor Speedway*);
Len taking an anniversary lap at the Indianapolis Motor Speedway in 2002, in the restored car he drove for a second place finish in 1962 (*photo courtesy of Gil Belamy*).
right:
Going into the first turn after taking the green flag, 1962 Indianapolis 500 (*photo courtesy of the Indianapolis Motor Speedway*).

Previous page:
An official qualifying photograph taken as a participant in the 1962 Indianapolis 500 (*photo courtesy of the Indianapolis Motor Speedway*).

©2002, Len Sutton

P. O. Box 19081
Portland, Oregon 97280

First Printing: November 2002   1,600 copies

Printed by Walsworth Publishing Company
Marceline, Missouri USA

ISBN 0-9725421-0-8

All rights reserved. This book may not be reproduced in whole or in part, by electronic or any other means which exists without the permission of the author.

My road to Indy

A Narrative by Len Sutton

Forward by Donald Davidson

Cover and Book Design
by Christy Sutton

Forward

by Donald Davidson
HISTORIAN,
INDIANAPOLIS MOTOR SPEEDWAY

A.J. Watson, Len Sutton, Donald Davidson and Rodger Ward

Of all the honors and privileges I have been blessed with over the years, I would have to say that having Len Sutton call up and ask me to write the forward for his book would rank among my most cherished.

I first became aware of Len sometime between late February and early March of 1957 when I obtained my very first Indianapolis 500 Yearbook, the 1956 edition. Born and raised in England, I had been aware of motor racing from my earliest recollection but it had never really grabbed me until the previous September. All of a sudden the subject of Grand Prix stats and history became the most important thing in my life. Why, I have no idea. All I know is that I read everything I could possibly get my hands on and it wasn't long before I stumbled upon a mysterious and fascinating thing called the Indianapolis 500.

I would regularly visit a used book store on my way home from school and I finally saved up enough pocket money to purchase a marvelous publication, containing a listing of the top three finishers in all of history's major races, including the 500. I was so captivated by the names of the latter that I discovered it took very little to be able to memorize the whole thing.

And when I read a review in a magazine of Floyd Clymer's latest publication, I prevailed upon my devoted and understanding mother to try and locate one on her next day trip to London. She was successful and my life was changed forever. A whole new world opened up for me.

One of the very first of the legion of brand new names revealed to me through the book was that of Len Sutton. He was a rookie that year and there is a shot of him in there, removing his rookie stripes and being congratulated by a fellow driver identified as Jim McWithey. It was, in fact, Len's long time friend Jack Turner, causing me to realize later on that not all of what I had read and memorized was entirely accurate!! There was also a line of copy in there which has stayed with me to this day. It describes Len's month-ending accident in which he landed upside down in Roger Wolcott's dirt car, quoting the doctor in decidedly NON-British dialogue, "We finally scraped enough rubber from his back to repair it." (Ouch !!)

All of which went towards convincing me what a bunch of tough nuts these Indianapolis 500 drivers had to have been. I was to gaze at a ton of headshots over the next few years and often wondered if there could possibly be a single approachable driver among them. Some of them looked decidedly ferocious and so what a complete surprise there was in store for me when I finally made it to the track in 1964 and met them. The majority were among the friendliest, happiest, warmest, most considerate and fulfilled people one could ever hope to meet. I was totally shocked as I had assumed that they would be extremely intense and snappy by the very nature of the pressures I assumed they were under.

My three-week stay at the track that first year defies description. I entered a fantasy world and was immediately taken into the inner circle of the participants. I met every conceivable driver, car owner, mechanic, official and press person imaginable. I made a list on the flight home of every driver I had met, past or present. The total was 83. Among the first was Len Sutton.

What a wonderful person he was. So humble, so courteous, so easy going, so self-effacing. I was amazed. How could this possibly be the same person who had finished second in the 500 just two years before and who had qualified yet again only a couple of hours before I met him? I had to pinch myself. Could this really be the same person who had won at Springfield and Milwaukee and who had been required to have all that rubber scraped from his back in '56? He was somebody I had been reading about for seven years and now here I was standing next to him, talking with him. And he was smiling and he was NICE!!

He was so thoughtful and analytical. His interests were many and he seemed just as happy talking about politics and world affairs as he was about racing. He seemed to enjoy discussions and it was interesting to watch him in a group because he was such a good listener. He'd sit on a tire, hug one knee and take it all in. Then somebody would make a statement to which he didn't entirely agree. He'd grin, clear his throat, squint with one eye and formulate what he was going to say. I noted that he always seemed to choose his words carefully and so it wasn't that much of a surprise when he became involved in Oregon state politics not long thereafter.

Another observation is that many of his racing anecdotes were not necessarily about himself but rather of his colleagues. One of my comments after reading the first draft of this book was that he had very little to say of a personal nature about holding off Tony Bettenhausen, his hero, to win his first race at Trenton, let alone any of the joy he must have experienced in finishing second at Indianapolis. Surely these were among the highlights of his professional life and I wanted to know a great deal more about what went on and what he felt. "Well," he said, in typical Len fashion, "I didn't want to appear as if I was gloating."

And I couldn't help shaking my head and chuckling to myself when he described the Eddie Sachs/Dave MacDonald tragedy of 1964 from his point of view while hardly mentioning himself other than to note that the driver directly in front of him had been killed, as had the driver directly behind him. "Len," I yelled over the phone in mock frustration, "Tell us what happened to YOU!!"

I was there the night in 1964 when he was inducted into the exclusive Autolite Pacemakers Club for drivers who had led the Indianapolis 500 and I believe I may have been among the first to learn that he was contemplating retirement. I had been hired by Henry Banks to work for the United States Auto Club as soon as the 1965 500 was over and after a race at Langhorne a month later, we learned that Len had told a friend on the way to the airport, "I think that was probably my last race." As indeed it was.

But a new career was just around the corner. Sid Collins had taken me on as a member of the Radio Network broadcast by this time (another dream come true) and we would talk on a regular basis. He called up one day during that first winter with the startling news that Freddie Agabashian, his driver analyst since 1959, was stepping down due to the fact that Autolite had become a major sponsor of the broadcast and Freddie was working for Champion. "So what would you think," continued Sid, "about Len Sutton?"

And back he came!! He also became associated with a local TV and radio station, WFBM. They had him running around the pits and garage area, taping interviews and reports for a radio show and he asked me if I would go on with him. (Wow!! Len Sutton wants to interview ME??) WFBM had a little trailer parked in the oiled gravel lot right next to the old garage area and so over we went. Len was like a kid with a brand new toy with the portable tape recorder they'd given him. "I'll do a test," he said, still trying to become comfortable with which buttons to press, "and if we mess up we can start over."

I had to pinch myself again. Not only was I now being *interviewed* by Len Sutton, but in a few days hence, in spite of having no formal training whatsoever between us, we would BOTH be on the worldwide 500 Radio Network broadcast with Sid!! I'd gone from listening to the race on the radio in England in 1963, to watching part of it from Len's pit in 1964, to being on the broadcast and talking about him in 1965, and now sharing mic time with him in 1966.

One of the risks one runs in attempting to present a more in-depth character study of someone is that the subject might take offense or be embarrassed at some point raised. I hope Len won't mind the observation that he has always come across as looking so youthful. I have seen him up on a stage on numerous occasions, accepting some honor, hand clasped over wrist and always with an almost angelic look of wide-eyed boyhood innocence and eagerness on his face.

And there is something quite endearing about the way he has worn a cap since retirement. During his racing days, he would tend to pull the peak down so that he would almost have to tip his head back to see out. But for the last 35 years or so, his cap has always been perched on the back of his head, the peak pointed up at a 45-degree angle and with a tuft of hair sticking out in the front, making him look for all the world like a kid on a Little League baseball team!!

Len visited the Speedway for a few days in May 2002, along with Anita, his wife of 55 years, and he took a few laps of honor in his second-place-finishing "roadster" of 40 years ago. He was 76 years old by this time, but you would never have known it. His eyes were gleaming, there was a grin on his face, and a boyish-looking shock of hair was poking out from beneath the peak of his tipped-back 500 Oldtimer's Club cap. He *still* looked like a kid getting ready to go out and play baseball.

I would like to dedicate these memories to anyone and everyone who would like to put him or her self in my shoes for those 20 wonderful years. It could also be dedicated to anyone who has expressed the desire and ambition to follow in my foot steps. This does not mean that I did it right. It just means that with my following a dream, and having had the success I've had, hundreds of people come to me and ask, "How could I get into racing and do what you did?"

My response has changed through the years, but today I tell them to start with a lot of money! That of course has changed through the years as ambition and the luck of being in the right place at the right time worked better back then.

I had and have lost a great many friends at race tracks across the country and while luck or the absence of it played a part, some credit has to be given to the sanctity of life and how we perceive it. Many drivers I knew never thought about life after racing. Leading and the thought of winning was their only objective. But taking the checkered flag means being there at the finish. We could do and live the very same thing in our lives every day. Finish what you start and do the very best that you possibly can along the way.

A dedication

Possibly my last drive around the Indy Brickyard this last May 2002.

Table of Contents

My Beginning Years	1925-45	p. 2
My First Racing Years	1946	6
	1947	8
	1948	10
	1949	12
My Northwest Years	1950-53	14
	1954	18
	1955	22
My USAC Years	1956	26
	1957	32
	1958	38
	1959	42
	1960	46
	1961	50
	1962	60
	1963	66
	1964	72
	1965	80
Life After Racing	1966-present	86
	My Gratitude	90
	Acknowledgements	91
	Credits	91
	Statistics	92
	Index	94

My squadron on Hawaii, arrow indicates my location.

The date is around November 1943...

and I am walking the beaches of Waikiki in Honolulu, Hawaii looking for a little action. I am here after joining the Navy in November of '42. This journey began with boot camp in San Diego; aircraft machinist mate school in Norman, Oklahoma; gunnery school in Purcell, Oklahoma and then shipped back to San Diego to be assigned to a flight squadron. After a couple of training sessions at both San Clemente Island and Long Beach, plus a stint in Jacksonville, Florida with PBY's, our Squadron, UTRON 7, would be the replacement for a utility aircraft group stationed on Ford Island at Pearl Harbor in Oahu, Hawaii.

On the beach in Hawaii

This is the aircraft I maintained as the flight engineer.

I was very fortunate in my Navy enlistment to be assigned to duties in aircraft as I had chosen aircraft studies in high school before enlisting.

There were several times during my enlistment when I felt challenged. I ended up being assigned as a crew chief on a PV1 (Army B-26). It was part of my regular duties to have my aircraft ready to fly at all times. Doing pre-flight inspections plus engine warm-ups was a daily routine. During those two years, there were times when a crew would be established to test an aircraft that had been out of commission for some time and when volunteers were asked to step forward, I was always first in line. We never lost an aircraft that I was assigned to, or even lost an engine when I was in charge. It still amazes me as I was just 17 and 18 at the time. I loved being in the hot seat.

You may wonder what this has to do with auto racing. Something within me has always required that there be a challenge ahead. Sometimes the challenge has been just to stay alive. This could date back to when I was just two years old and fell in a post hole that was being dug when we lived on the Oregon coast. The 14-inch hole was about 20 feet deep and intended for a utility pole. The hand auger that was being used was left in place and when I fell in I got lodged about half-way down. They tried to pull the auger out but that didn't work. They finally decided to dig another deep hole along side to get me out. I guess I was crying all the time but I never gave up.

> "**S**omething within me has always required that there be a challenge ahead. Sometimes the challenge has been just to stay alive."

This clipping appeared in the newspaper after my accident. (1927)

Infant Falls in New Well, Buried Two Hours in Dirt

GLENEDEN, Or., Aug. 11.—Two hours' imprisonment in a well on the ranch of Mr. and Mrs. L. S. Sutton has evidently had little effect on Leonard, their two-year-old son. The well was 20 feet deep but the augur for boring was still in position. The infant fell eight feet and was buried in dirt and sand for more than two hours.

How about when I was six and my older brother knocked me over backwards with a pitch fork? He hit the front of my skull with the tine as I reached over to get something on the ground while he worked with the hay. It missed my right eye by a quarter inch. Half an inch lower and a tine would have gone clear into my skull. I still have a dent in my forehead where the pitchfork landed. There may not have been a challenge here but if I were a cat with nine lives — I'd used up two of mine.

left:
My sister Shirley (two years older) and my younger brother Jim (by three years), circa 1930.

right:
I am standing on the left, in front of my cousin Chet. My older brother Ron is standing behind our younger brother Jim, circa 1934.

*B*orn in 1925 and raised during the Depression . . .

often makes a person a little conservative with the buck. I always had a couple of jobs. By the sixth grade I had a paper route earning $1.16 a month, and trapped muskrats and pelted them making five cents a pelt. I don't think I was ever considered lazy. Even today, I am still proud of the fact that I have never been unemployed and have never drawn an unemployment check.

In my youth, while living in Clackamas just south of Portland, Oregon, I had my first exposure to auto racing. I attended what was supposed to be a midget auto race at Kelly Field in Oregon City. It was a softball field. As I remember, it ended up being called off because only six cars showed up. In later years I learned that one of those racers was none other than Gordy Youngstrom, who I was to race against many times.

My other exposure to auto racing was at the Canby fair, where they had a Model "T" race on a half-mile dirt track. The thing I still remember is the drivers steering with their right hand and using their left hand to hold the throttle and the spark handles together as they drove around the track. You can not appreciate this unless you have seen a model T throttle and spark configuration.

In 1945, my regular Navy days came to an end and I was shipped back stateside to be discharged from the Navy. I arrived at Bremerton, Washington about Christmas time 1945. I could hardly wait to get back to Portland and take up where I'd left off. Soon after my discharge, I started taking flying lessons, but by the time I was soloing there didn't seem to be enough action to keep my interest. The car I was driving at the time was a 1930 Model A roadster. No fenders, no top, but it did have a 1936 Ford V-8 engine. I used to burn rubber every time I took off . . . that is if the law wasn't around. My friend from grade school, Gordon Janzck, asked me one day if I wanted to go out to Portland Speedway with him and watch a roadster race. I'll admit I hadn't even heard of roadster races. I believe we went out in my roadster and up into the grandstands we went. It wasn't too long before I was hooked. I told Gordon, "I bet I could do that." Keep in mind that while in the Navy I had basically no driving opportunities and in the six or eight months since my discharge I had maybe a thousand miles under my belt. Experience didn't come to mind at that time. I still had my mind made up.

After the race my friend and I went down and struck up a conversation with the participants. Before long we had the needed invitation. I was assigned a number to put on the car, told to install a seat belt, bring a helmet and be out there the next Sunday. I don't remember where I got a helmet, but I do remember wiring my dad's old leather belt into the seat.

I am leading the race. Note the windshield posts still in place.

By my second race, I had a sponsor on the side of the car.

This photo is of my first day of racing. This is my second race. I'm in the lead here, but I believe I finished second.

In my very first race . . .

one incident sticks in my mind. When the race was over, I remember this guy came up to me and says, "What the %#@* were you trying to do when I started to pass? Run me off the track??" I replied, "What am I supposed to do to keep you from passing??" I thought that was the way you did it. The fact is, I didn't have as much experience as the average 15-year-old has today. When I arrived at the race track that day it showed. Honestly, at age 21, I was that naive about racing.

In the next race, the class B event, I finished second. By now, I was really hooked. There were only two races left for the '46 racing season. I believe I ended up in the blackberry bushes in the final race of that year. Anita, the love of my life, did not like my car or my racing and because we were going to get married by the end of the year, I guess I felt the car had to go. With no top, it really was a summer thing. Besides, I found out there were more cars than there were drivers, so I could drive someone else's race car.

The excitement of driving race cars was what I wanted, not the chores of working on them. The 1947 roadster season found me looking for a ride and because I had two races under my belt, I felt I had something to offer. Leroy Weedmeyer had a shop just a few blocks from where we lived and had a roadster with no driver. It was a natural for me to have that ride. We had varied success, but by mid-season I wanted a car with more power. Don Turner drove his own car with more power than he could handle and I convinced him "I could get it done." I got the ride but found out shortly that the handling was not up to the power of the engine. I crashed twice and found myself out of a ride.

> "*This is where I ended my second race . . . in the blackberry bushes.*"

Vollstedt's first race car. A "T" pick-up powered by a Lincoln Zepher V-12.

Now appearing on the scene was none other than Rolla Vollstedt. He had purchased a roadster racer, owned by his boss and when he showed up at the race track, his driver Frankie McGowen, decided he needed a different ride. Dick Martin, an owner with Bob Gregg as the driver, told Vollstedt that a guy by the name of Sutton had just lost his ride and with a little luck he might make himself into a driver. As luck would have it, I got the nod. We were unable to finish that race but Rolla and I hit it off and I had a ride for the next season.

Rolla credits a lot of his early success to George "Pop" Koch who was the person who actually built the car. It was a 1925 "T" pick-up with a Lincoln V-12 engine. With all the trouble we encountered that day, Pop Koch encouraged Rolla to let him take the car home with him for the winter and he would make it a winner. Pop took out the V-12 and put in a Merc engine. With a few other changes we found a winning combination and won the championship the following year.

1947 began an era of innovations...

as local racers were taking note of differences like engine location and tires, and began adapting those ideas. Competition was heating up with the addition of drivers such as Jack McGrath and Manuel Ayulo up from California. They ran a race at Portland Speedway, broke the track record and ran one-two very handily.

Race promoter J.C. Agajanian leans over the car to speak to me before the start of a race at Carrell Speedway near Los Angeles.

GREINER

This is the match race between me and Allen Heath.

There were many other drivers who had as much or more experience than I had. Drivers like McGowen and Gregg were two but there were others like Palmer Crowell, Gordy Youngstrom, Howard Osborne, Max Humm, "Wild" Bill Hyde, Andy Wilson, Don Moore, Jim Martin and Randy Francis that were probably as good or better than myself. Ernie Koch started racing about the same time as I did and until I left the area, we ended up being the drivers to beat. He probably won as many local races and championships as I did. Randy Francis was hard to beat when driving Blackie Blackburn's roadster. Randy's future destiny of being a top local Ford dealer took him out of the weekly roadster racing we all learned to enjoy.

While most of our racing took place in Oregon, we found that traveling north to Seattle every other week gave us more exposure - plus an added income. We raced on the Aurora quarter-mile paved track in northern Seattle. Rolla claims we took home between three and four hundred dollars every week we went up there. Washington cars and drivers were very competitive and beating them was not a slam dunk.

Bob Donker and Phil Foubert were always there and did not like Oregon cars and drivers coming into their back yard and taking home the bacon. We probably won maybe half the races we ran up there. I do remember one of the races was a double header, where they ran a full race program of midgets and roadsters. At that race Allen Heath, a top midget driver, had fast time in the midgets and I had fast time in the roadsters. The promoter thought a match race between the two of us would be rather exciting. As I remember, it *was* rather exciting.

Salem, Oregon quarter-mile paved track where we raced on Friday nights.

Probably the most excited person was Vollstedt because even though Allen out qualified me in the time trials, Rolla thought I should be able to beat him. They had us run two three-lap events with me on the pole in one event and with Heath on the pole in the other. Allen, a more experienced driver and a clown to boot, kind of played with me, getting his midget so close I couldn't even see him at times. In the end he beat me both times and Vollstedt still grimaces today whenever it comes up. He thought I gave up too easily.

Myself, Jack Greiner, Don Waters, and Rolla (far right) with the bill cap turned up in Gardena, California, October 30, 1948.

Leaving Portland Speedway for California...

In 1948, after the season was over in the northwest, Rolla and I took his car down to Los Angeles to run a couple of races. The first weekend we raced at Huntington Beach. This was a quarter-mile paved track. They ran what they called "split 50's." The odd- and even-qualified cars went into two 50-lap feature events. Troy Ruttman won in one feature and I won the other. The second was Carrell Speedway, a half-mile dirt track where Ruttman "cut his teeth." Other drivers there that day were Jack McGrath, Jimmy Davies, Red Amick, Joe James, Bob Scott, Andy Linden, Dick Rathmann, Pat Flaherty, Don Freeland and Allen Heath. These were future Indy drivers. After tapping the wall during the early running with Rolla's car, I jumped into Don Waters' car, from Salem, Oregon and qualified for the feature. I remember running with Ruttman and Heath during that event but do not remember where, or even if, I finished.

By this time it was evident there were other types of racing besides roadsters. I started showing up at the midget races. My first midget was

above: Portland Speedway during a race, circa 1949.

right: My fourth midget ride was this front wheel creation with an Offy engine.

"*This was the ultimate. The car was very interesting but was scary to drive. I got to appreciate Offy power.*"

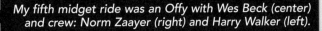

My fifth midget ride was an Offy with Wes Beck (center) and crew: Norm Zaayer (right) and Harry Walker (left).

powered by a Star engine and was again owned by Leroy Weedmeyer. One race was all we got with that engine. We moved up to a Solar with a Ford V8-60 power plant. Several races later I was in Joe Hoag's midget and we were looking better all the time. Before the season was over I heard that a Jim Soukup was building a front-wheel-drive midget and it was going to be powered by an Offenhauser.

This was the ultimate. I was asked if I'd be interested and of course I said yes. The car was very interesting but was scary to drive. I soon learned it would win the helmet dash, but by main event time it would break - I believe I lost eight wheels in seven races.

At least I got to appreciate Offy power and was able to get a wonderful Offy-powered midget for the '49 season with Wes Beck.

My second midget ride was a Solar with Leroy Weedmeyer.

My third midget ride was a V-8/60 owned by Joe Hoag. I'm in No. 65 and Mel McGaughy is in the No. 22 car.

During this time I had a regular five-day a week job with the Oregon Air National Guard at the air base. I was the propeller specialist and worked on P-51's and DC-3's. More than once Rolla would bring his roadster out to the air base and we would test it up and down the taxi strips. I believe in '49 or '50, when my three-year air guard enlistment was up, the commander, Colonel Doolittle, advised me that in the future, Sundays would be instruction days and not absent days (going racing). I didn't re-up and found another regular job. You can tell by this time how important racing was to me.

Wes Beck and I stayed together for several seasons and we won the Oregon Midget Championship in 1950. This car was a Richter chassis and was not very new, so Wes went to California and bought a Kurtis. He now had two midget race cars. Gordy Youngstrom drove the Richter and I drove the new one. I really believe the Richter was the better car.

Anita and I started a family . . .

and whenever possible we took our young daughter with us when we went racing. The exception was the out of town races when the family usually stayed home.

At Portland Speedway with Anita and our first daughter, Christy. In the background is my friend Gordon Janzck and his wife, Mary.

Still looking for that challenge, I wanted to try my hand at stock cars and what we called big cars.

While I placed pretty well in stock cars, I never won a race in the northwest. By this time I was working for Francis Ford, a local Ford dealership, and I convinced them to give me a current model Ford two-door. We stripped it down and raced it. My best finish in the West coast was third place at Bay Meadows in Burl Jackson's 1951 Oldsmobile. During the race I flipped the car but we got it back on it's wheels and stayed in the race to get that third-place finish. A big name at that time, Hershel McGriff, finished fourth.

In big cars, Vollstedt would just put a funny looking tail on his roadster and we would show up and race. When we started winning these races they changed the rules so we could not compete in the roadster. That's when Rolla built a true big car to make us legal so we could run with the others.

We won the Portland Meadows' major event three out of four times running. This

above and right: Burl's Olds before I flipped it and as I flipped it.

was an annual event, with lots of prize money. By the time we added up lap prizes, leading the race and then winning it also, we may have won $1,500 total. Winnings from that event gave us enough to put a down payment on our first house. WOW, we were going to be home owners!

We were still racing the roadster and won the roadster championship in '51, '52 and '53. Rolla developed an exceptional engine that was a GMC "bottom end" with a Horning head for the top. That engine had a horsepower and torque combination that was unbeatable.

Rolla Vollstedt's big car as we get ready to race at Portland Meadows. From the left, after me, is Rolla, Pop Koch, Homer Norman and Bill Devecka.

Racing at Playland quarter-mile paved track in Seattle on a Friday night. I'm in the No. 27 and Harold Sperb is behind me in the No. 55 car.

THORSEN

Sometime during those early 50's years . . .

Del McClure, from Portland, asked me if I would like to drive his big car in a couple of races at Calistoga, California. It was a half-mile dirt track where the California boys had command. Del's DeSoto-powered rig was always in the running on the Oregon circuit but not as quick as Vollstedt's car. We arrived with anticipation but had no idea how we would stack up.

In the end we had fast time, started last, and won both nights. It was a two-day affair. I heard 20 years later that we still held the 10-lap heat race track record.

I remember another time in 1952 when the final roadster race of the season was coming up at Portland Speedway and the Championship was at stake.

I was in Vollstedt's Horning GMC and we had quick time in qualifying. The Washington roadsters were there too and it appeared that both the Oregon and Washington Championships were at stake. Ernie Koch and I were probably neck and neck for the Oregon Championship. In the heat race we "spun a spool" in the rear end, putting us out of the race and the championship unless something drastic happened. One of my close friends, but also a competitor, Harold Sperb came up to me and said, "How would you like my ride for the rest of the day?" He drove his own car all the time except when something like this would happen. I remembered he had helped me out like this once before.

As you can imagine, I accepted and was now excited all over again. Harold had qualified sixth, but they started me last in the 100-lap feature and I finished third. Shorty Templeman was the winner. With all the points that were scored in that race, Shorty earned the Washington Champ title and I was the Oregon Champ.

The promoter then believed there should be a Northwest Champion and he put the top four Washington finishing cars and the top four Oregon finishing cars in a 20-lap run off. I ended up winning that race and it was about as exciting a finish as you could ask for in one season of racing.

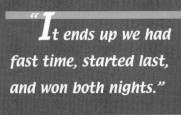

"*It ends up we had fast time, started last, and won both nights.*"

above, left:
Del McClure and me at Calistoga, California half-mile dirt track.

top right:
I'm leading this run-off in Harold Sperb's car at Portland Speedway.

center right:
Running at Aurora quarter-mile in Seattle on a Friday night.

bottom right:
Harold (in No. 66) and me (in No. 3) dicing it out at Playland in Seattle.

> "**H**omer had a gorgeous red No. 55 Kurtis that I found very easy to win with."

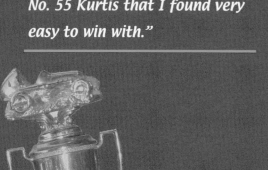

In about 1953 I decided to change my midget ride from Wes Beck to Homer Norman of Kirkland, Washington. I won the Oregon Championship with Homer's great midget in both 1954 and '55.

I remember one of those years, Louie Sherman and I were tied for the Championship going into the last race of the season. I won the race and the Oregon title. I believe I was second to Mel McGaughy in both those years in Washington. We also took the car to California for several races each fall and we finished in the top three spots several times.

In the summer of 1954 my good friend Blackie Blackburn of Portland lined me up with Ranald Ferguson of Bickelton, Washington. He owned a 1953 Lincoln which ran third in the '53 Mexican Road race with Jack McGrath as the driver. I was asked if I was interested in driving the Mexican Road race in 1954. It took me five seconds to answer "yes" to that question. With the racing season pretty much over at home, Blackie and I took the '53 Lincoln McGrath had driven, down to watch the AAA Indy-type race at Sacramento. Blackie had been to Indy as a "stooge" for Herb Porter in previous years, so Blackie knew some of the people. We enjoyed the race, I got to meet some new racing people and then we headed home.

ARN-JAY

right:
A picture I took as the drivers were getting ready to start the Sacramento race in 1954. From left is Jerry Hoyt, Jimmy Bryan, Bob Sweikert, Jimmy Reece, Rodger Ward, Johnny Boyd and Edgar Elder.

opposite page, far left:
I have just received a trophy for winning the dash.

opposite page, middle:
Homer Norman and me after winning the race and trophy.

opposite page, right:
Mel McGaughy and me at Playland in Seattle.

This was, of course, before freeways and it was not easy to make good time. That wasn't going to stop me from trying though, and eight hours and 20 minutes later we were stopped at a road block just outside Portland and were taken 50 miles back to Salem. The State Police officer told us they had been trying to catch us for some time and it had taken a road block to do it. They couldn't catch us from behind. I guess we averaged about 79 mph from Sacramento to Portland (650 miles). We did have a couple of pit stops and a quick sandwich along the way.

This is the car, just the way it looked when we drove to Sacramento to watch a race in 1954.

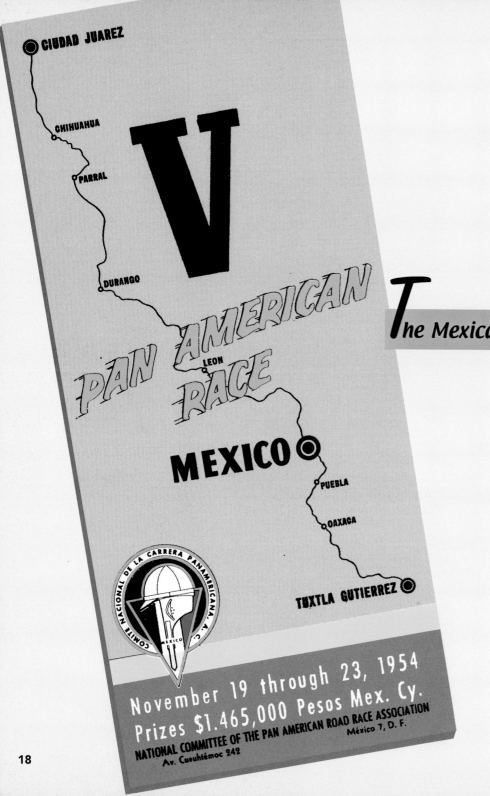

*T*he Mexican Road Race was a world of its own.

We left Portland over a month before the actual start itself. We drove the '53 Lincoln, our practice car, and towed the '54 Lincoln on a flatbed truck. The support crew were in separate cars. After arriving in Ciudad Juárez Mexico, Ranald and I started our practice runs up and down the Mexican highways.

I believe this is the old race car Ranald drove in the Tri-Cities area.

loose in a candy store. I was to drive as close to race speeds as I could while Ranald was accumulating all the data we would need for the actual race. The Mexican police would maybe wave or turn their heads as we went by. The race itself was almost a national holiday but even in practice everyone cheered us on. There were five legs, averaging maybe 350 miles per leg for a total distance of 1908 miles.

The start of the third leg began in Mexico City and when we arrived, the local kids just stormed us. They were all over the car every time we stopped. When we got ready to bed down for the night, I

We began in Chihuahua, which was the start of the last leg and drove like hell back to the last-day finish line, Ciudad Juárez. With me practicing, Ranald would take notes of speeds and hazardous turns. For the next two or three weeks we did this daily. For me it was like being turned

Cuidad Juárez
Chihuahua
Durango
Mexico City
Oaxaca
Tuxtla Gutiérrez

> "Ranald and I started our practice runs up and down the Mexican highways...it was like being turned loose in a candy store."

Ranald at the wheel of his 1953 Lincoln.

remember a couple of the kids were yelling, "We watch your car, we watch your car." We mistakenly said, "We're OK" and it wasn't until the next morning we understood what they really meant. The race car was broken into and most everything was gone, including our racing helmets. Somehow we replaced them. All our camera equipment was also stolen, resulting in the loss of all our pictures.

We are in Mexico with a crew member and a support vehicle.

A photo shoot with the '54 Lincoln. To the left of Ran and me is one of our sponsors, Ed Francis of Francis Lincoln/Mercury.

THE OREGONIAN

Everything went pretty well after that until we arrived in Oaxaca (finishing town for the first leg). We decided it was time to bring the '54 Lincoln (our racing car) off the flatbed and start practicing with it. We were at about 5,000 feet elevation and the engine settings had been done in Portland, which is 500 feet elevation. It was late afternoon as we tried again and again to depart Oaxaca for our trip down to the starting line city, Tuxtla Gutiérrez. The engine was detonating with too much spark advance or too lean a mixture.

When we finally got started to Tuxtla, it was turning dark. I did not take into account that our previous runs were all daytime and, of course, I had never been on this road before and we were in a different car.

Running at speeds of 80 to 100 MPH, we were on a lonely highway with little traffic but often with sightings of animals.

On a straight stretch and coming over an undulation my headlights caught maybe 10 or 15 head of cattle.

In trying to miss them, I got too far onto the left shoulder of the highway and lost it in the gravel. We ended up in a ravine (right side up) with the headlights

A stop along the way while in Mexico with one of the support cars.

still burning. A while later some Mexicans found us, helped us out of the car and dragged us up to the highway. We appeared conscious and not bloody, but I had broken vertebrae and Ranald had several cracked ribs. Although they were trying to be helpful, as they hauled me up the hill my butt was bouncing on the

left:
Another shot of Ran and me before I crashed.

this page:
Checkered flag for a sports car at one of the legs of the Mexican Road Race.

> "*I* remember when Dad had his torso cast on, I was the only one with an arm small enough and long enough to reach down inside the cast to scratch his back."
>
> –Christy, Len's daughter

rocks and every time I yelled they just went faster.

When we finally made it up to the road they set me down. That's when the ants started crawling all over me. Yes, the biting kind. It actually took my mind off of my back, which by then was really hurting. Within a half hour our crew arrived and then it was a trip on down to Tuxtla to a hospital. I use the word "hospital" loosely! It was an open air cot where the kids stood at the window and just stared and giggled.

It was finally decided that I had to be taken to Mexico City if I was to get any medical attention. The crew, which included Dick Wilson, Dick Ringer and Dick Kessinger, took me to their motel and wrapped me up in a bed sheet. Kessinger tells me today that the Bardahl people had access to a Douglas DC3 which eventually took me to Mexico City. Bardahl was one of our sponsors and Francis Lincoln/Mercury was the other.

I barely remember the DC3 trip except that as I lay flat on the floor of the airplane, it felt like I was going to explode. The sheet was so snugly wrapped around me that the gas building up inside of me had no where to go. They finally cut the sheet off to give me room to breathe.

Once we got to Mexico City I had a cast installed from armpit to hip and was advised that after it dried, if I could stand up and walk, they would release me. Twenty-four hours later I was on a commercial airliner flying back to Portland and wore a full body cast for the next four months.

A perfected GMC with a Horning head...

made 1955 a very interesting and successful year for me. We were almost unbeatable. Racing had come far enough along in the Northwest, where there were at least two or three Offy engines (the kind they used at Indianapolis) competing against us. I believe there were about 12 big car races that year and Vollstedt claims we won 10 of them.

Standing with Pat Vidan at the start/finish line after winning a three-lap helmet dash.

Of course we won the Championship but after the season was winding down, Vollstedt decided to make a deal with one of our friendly competitors. He asked to borrow an Offy engine for the race in Sacramento that fall and make an attempt to qualify in the AAA Indy-type race held there. In that type of race the Offy was so superior that no other engine was even used.

We had to stretch the wheel base four inches on our car to meet the specs for that race. The engine we borrowed was new at the start of the 1954 season but had not been overhauled after two seasons of racing. There were 23 cars on hand at Sacramento trying to make the 18-car field. We qualified eighth, meaning that only seven Indianapolis class drivers out-qualified us.

This was a tremendous thrill for us, just to be in the lineup. The year before we were just spectators. Now we were IN it, along with defending National Champion, Jimmy Bryan, and Bob Sweikert, who had just won Indianapolis in May.

The race started and were just holding our own, when a rear radius rod broke, putting us out of the race after 21 laps. The engine was blowing oil out of the breathers so bad, I had already used up all my cover lenses (maybe six) so I could not have gone another five laps anyway.

Don Collins, who was with Vollstedt and me at Sacramento, took the engine apart after returning to Portland, completely rebuilding it. A couple of weeks later I went to Phoenix and again qualified to make the field. Of the group that went to Sacramento, only Don and I were able to make the trip to Phoenix so it was just the two of us. Don and I did the whole thing. Don has reminded me in later years that we towed the race car to Phoenix

Rolla and me with George "Pop" Koch as the car is about to be stretched to meet the requirements to run at the AAA event in Sacramento.

using the stock car I was driving for Francis Ford, the people I worked for. We put a trailer hitch on it, hooked up the trailer and away we went. I'm still amazed that between just the two of us we got the car ready for practice, qualifying, and the start of the race.

At this race there were 28 cars and drivers hoping to make the starting field. With only 18 starting positions for the race, 10 were going to miss the show. I qualified twelfth right between Pat O'Connor and Jimmy Bryan.

Of course, making the race and then finishing 100 miles is another thing. Ten or 15 miles into the race, I already had to make a early pit stop. The throttle arm came loose and the engine went to an idle. Don got that fixed in a hurry and I went back out. At about the halfway mark the fuel gauge, which had "alcy" going to it to show fuel pressure, burst and was spewing fuel all over my face and goggles, so I came in again. Don flipped up the hood to see if there was anything he could do to fix it, and the AAA official came over and made a back and forth motion, like cutting off your breath at your Adam's apple. Don looked over at him like "Just give me a second and I will fix it" and the official shows him this sign again, indicating he really meant it. Yes, that meant we were through for the day. But there is a good part to this story. I was offered an Indianapolis ride for the next year based on that Sacramento and Phoenix driving performance.

With Blackie Blackburn working for Herb Porter and the Wolcott team, I was selected to be their driver for next year.

This was at Portland Speedway. When we took Rolla's GMC-powered sprint car to Sacramento in September, this car was stretched four inches in the wheelbase and we borrowed a well-used 270 Offy engine. This was my passport to Indy.

"*The good part of this story is that I was offered an Indianapolis ride for the next year based on my driving performance at Sacramento and Phoenix.*"

Here we are lined up to start the race at Phoenix. This was the last AAA Championship race ever held. Don Collins is in the dark t-shirt. The No. 29 car to my left is Pat O'Connor and behind him is the Dean Van Lines Special driven by Jimmy Bryan, the eventual winner. Notice the four-inch extension to the hood of my car.

In late April 1956, with my helmet bag in tow and a lot of pride and enthusiasm, I was heading to *"the greatest spectacle in racing,"* the Indianapolis 500. I had worked out all winter and at about 160 pounds, I had a set of arms and shoulder muscles that I was proud of. I could do 17 one-arm push ups with my right arm and 12 with my left. When I arrived at Indy, I saw the biggest arena I had ever seen in my life. It was breathtaking.

Packing up and heading for Indianapolis . . .

A promotional shoot with Tony Hulman, then President of the Indianapolis Motor Speedway seated in a '56 pace car.

The race car lineup is Rodger Ward on the left, Pat Flaherty middle and me on the right. Pat ended up winning the 500 that year.

My car was a Roger Wolcott-owned, Herb Porter-crew chiefed and Blackie Blackburn "stooged" dirt track-type car.

These types of car had been used previously at Indy, but by 1956 the Kurtis-type roadster had them all but replaced. Mine and about three others out of 56 cars, were the only older types.

The first order of business for the month of May was for rookies like myself to take a driver's test. Jack Turner and I were two out of seventeen rookies to take this test. Jack and I both passed and we went on to have our practice runs and work up to speed. The regulars were running in the low 140's and I was managing 138 and 139.

This was a significant moment. After passing my rookie test, I could remove the "rookie stripe" off the back of my car. My great friend and northwest driver, Jack Turner, looks on.

"*Once*, about mid-month, I spun it coming off the number two turn. I never hit anything, fortunately, but I can say it scared the crap out of me."

First Believed Dead, Sutton Is In Fair Condition

By JEP CADOU JR.
Star Sports Editor

Rookie Driver Len Sutton miraculously escaped death yesterday when his Wolcott Special rolled over twice in the fourth of a rash of Speedway mishaps on the eve of what seems sure to be the fastest day of qualifications in 500-Mile Race history.

The 30-year-old Sutton, Portland (Ore.) driver who took the first spin of Speedway practice back on May 3, was coming out of the northeast turn when his red-and-white speedster got too high, nearly hit the wall and started sliding sideways.

It rolled over twice and finally came to rest on its wheels in the infield 1,000 feet from where the slide began.

SUTTON was at first believed dead by observers on the scene but recovered consciousness on arrival at Methodist Hospital. Attendants said his condition was fair and he escaped with a badly lacerated hand, track burns and no apparent fractures.

"I really don't know what happened," Sutton told The Star from the emergency room at the hospital. "I haven't the slightest idea. I was running along on the track and the next thing I know I woke up in this room here."

Drivers Do[n] Angeles and Haddonfield, injury when wall and E[d]mond was spun. All haps occu[rred] the south tradition[al] gerous track.

The rest of the month went along so-so. The Friday before the first weekend of qualifying about 15 minutes before the track closed for the day, Herb ask me to take the car out to see if we could get it up over the 140 mark. I remember a local Portland driver, Gordy Youngstrom was there in the garage with us on that day and I was pleased to take the car out and let him see me run. The next thing I remember was waking up in the Methodist Hospital with my right hand bandaged and a real bad headache. I'd flipped coming out of the third turn, landing on my head and shoulder, grinding off the

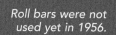
Roll bars were not used yet in 1956.

INDIANAPOLIS MOTOR SPEEDWAY

Northwest drivers Shorty Templeman, Jack Turner, and myself with Sid Collins of the Speedway network.

back of my helmet and scraping a quarter inch of hide off my back and the back of my right hand. I also had a broken shoulder. I guess I was unconscious for some time. They ended up having to perform grafts on the back of my right hand.

My first trip to Indy was a disaster. Anita had stayed in Portland during that time, but came back to rescue me. Although I remained in the hospital for a couple of weeks, Tony Hulman had an ambulance bring Anita and me to the track on race day and we watched the race from his favored seating area. Rolla also came back after my accident and was sitting with us. The only thing I vividly remember is Paul Russo having his tire blow out right in front of us. Several weeks later we traveled back to Portland.

Every year at Indy, each race entrant was given a silver badge that allowed him entrance and unlimited access to all areas of the track. I have badges from my rookie year all the way through to 2002. As an "honored" past driver, I also received badges during those years I worked as a broadcaster or anytime that I attended the race.

Over the years, these badges have become valuable collector items.

As I got back on my feet and regained my strength and confidence back in Portland, Vollstedt had a race car available for me to drive and I ran a few races that summer.

That fall, Don Collins had a big car owned by Minnie Miller and it was ready to go to Sacramento for the annual Champ car race. They didn't have a driver.

This race car was one of the old Blue Crowns which had dominated Indy in the 40's. It originally had independent front suspension, but was now modified with a solid front axle. It was a pavement and Indy-type car and should never have been on a dirt track. I was asked and again I accepted the opportunity to compete with the big boys. We qualified 18th and within a dozen or so laps from the start another car stalled in front of me. I hit him and ended up in the fence.

Hardwood Door midget No. 8 in Florida during the Tangerine tournament.

Soon after that, Bob Gregg called me. He had gone back east to drive midgets for Ashley Wright of Hardwood Door along with Shorty Templeman, who had been driving for Ashley for some time.

They had a car with no driver and a big seasonal race was coming up at the West 16th Street Speedway track across from the Indy 500. Shorty was in one car, Gregg in another and I landed a ride in the third car.

This midget race track was probably the most prestigious of its kind. The night before the 500 they would sometimes run three full events. I had never been there before but a quarter-mile paved track is just that and you attack it like any other track. Warm ups went well and in my qualifying attempt I set a new track record. When the track was torn down several years later, my track record was still standing. In the 100-lap feature, starting last and still not in the best physical condition, I got tired before it was over and I finished back a ways.

My performance landed me a steady ride with them and we went on to do a winter circuit in Florida after that. Before arriving in Florida, the crew stopped in Los Angeles to pick up a newly-developed

Sacramento with the Blue Crown in 1956.

> "West 16th Street Speedway was probably the most prestigious midget track of its kind."

Kurtis "roadster" midget for Gregg to drive and they had my midget ride with them too. There was a race scheduled at Bonnelli Stadium in Saugus, California, a quarter-mile paved, and Bob and I were to drive our cars there. Gregg had fast time but got in the wall in the helmet dash, putting him out. I went on to place second in the 100-lap feature race. Still working our way toward Florida, we stopped in Phoenix to run a midget race.

Once in Florida we set up camp in a mansion-type property that had empty stables and a six-car garage that was perfect for working on race cars. Ashley Wright had leased the place for the winter and there must have been a dozen of us living there.

We had 12 or 14 races in Florida that winter. I don't remember doing all that well and I know I never won any.

Here I am in the Hardwood Door midget No. 2 that I drove at Saugus, California.

In 1957, I packed up my family and headed for the Midwest. Anita and I were blessed to have two daughters now. Christy was nine and Hollie was four. Christy was still in school. We took her out of the fourth grade, packed our belongings,

jumped in our '50 Ford and headed East.

All I had was a midget ride and the prospect of a sprint car ride and with that we could hardly buy groceries and pay the rent.

I had never seen the sprint ride but knew it was in Dayton, Ohio and if we arrived by Saturday, I would transfer into Bill Cowgill's station wagon and I would leave immediately for Williams Grove, Pennsylvania to drive in my first race for Bill on Sunday.

Portland, Oregon

right:
My first sprint car race in Williams Grove, Pennsylvania. Car owned by Bill Cowgill.

below:
Same car at Terre Haute, Indiana.

Jim McWithey and me in Bill Cowgill's No. 27 at the half-mile high bank track in Salem, Indiana.

Anita had a brother and sister-in-law in Kokomo, Indiana. He was a fighter pilot in the Air Force and knew we were coming east. After we arrived in Dayton, Anita asked, "Which way is Kokomo, Indiana?" and I tell her it's kind of back in the direction we came from. Left on her own with two small children, this brave women then turned the car around and headed back down the road west until she arrived in Kokomo. Her brother rescued her and the kids. To this day, I'm still reminded of that trip.

The race at Williams Grove ended up being a race I'd like to forget.

As I mentioned, our family spent three to four days on the road getting to Dayton and then I slept in the back of a station wagon while Bill Cowgill towed the race car to the Grove. Race cars were already warming up as we arrived. I rubbed my eyes, asked where I could get a cup of hot coffee and tried to wake up. By the time I got my driving togs on and gathered my helmet, they had the car ready to go out for practice and warm up.

At this race track (or any other) you get your car warmed up and when the flagman gives everyone the green, everybody stands on it. By the time I'd reached the second turn, I had spun out. They re-started me with a push truck and two turns later I had spun out again. This time they just pushed me back to the pits.

Elmer George, the father of Tony George, was in the pit area. He had driven this same car for Cowgill earlier and was familiar with it. Bill asked him if he would take it out and see if there was anything wrong. By the second turn, he had spun it out just like I had. I can still hear the announcer's words over the public address, "Well, Sutton's back out and he's spun out again." I could have died right on the spot.

As it turns out, the car had been set up to run a high-bank /pavement track. It only had about a 15-degree turning radius in the steering. Most dirt cars had at least a 45 degree turning radius. Today's dirt cars

From left, Ed Elisian in No. 83, Jim McWithey in No. 33, I'm in No. 27 and Don Branson is in No. 98.

have about 70 degrees. Anyway, I don't remember what happened after that, but I'm sure I didn't qualify for the race.

I finally got back together with my family and we headed for Speedway to look for a place to live. I know a sensible person would have had the living arrangements all set, but with my loving wife and family, we just forged ahead and got it done. We found a duplex to rent and looked for some used furniture. Within a couple of days we had the kids in school, we were eating "three squares" and sleeping in our own beds. The month of May was in front of us and the Indy race track was almost right across the street.

While there were probably a few Midget races to run, my greatest interest was in finding a ride for the 500. I would leave every morning, go over to the track and just drop into every garage that had a door open.

I wasn't the only driver looking for a break into the big leagues. Many showed up at the race track and one of them was a young hot shot named A.J. Foyt. He was

above:
Terre Haute sprinters. I'm in No. 27, outside position, second row.

left:
Here is a promotional shot with owner, Bill Cowgill on the right. We are at the Salem half-mile high bank track.

only 21 years old but thought he knew it all. I remember he and his wife Lucy came by our duplex for a visit and although I knew A.J. a little before, after a couple of hours of hearing his version of racing, I did my best to try to ignore him. As he talked of how good he was and what he thought his prospects of being great were, I worked even harder at ignoring him. As you can imagine we both thought we were better than the other, but as time went on he proved that he was right. My attitude toward A.J. came back to bite me later. We were never close even though we were both rookies at Indy in 1958 and ran side by side in many races. I don't believe he ever forgot how I treated him in those early years. He nicknamed me "pork chop" and to this day he still jabs me with that nickname.

The year before, I got to know maybe a dozen mechanics, team members and drivers, plus there were maybe four to six cars without a driver at the Speedway and that is where I spent the most time. I'll never forget, as the month wore on, some of those garages had such little activity that cobwebs hung across the ceiling. I wore a crew cut and one day I got into one of those cobwebs and as I talked I kept trying to get the cobwebs out of my hair. I'm sure to this day they thought I was a little dingy. As it turned out, I never did land a ride for the 500 that year and the best I could do was make sure the night before the 500 I had my midget ready for the West 16th Street show.

It was a double race night and there was qualifying, helmet dashes, heats and a feature in each event. Chuck Rodee and I both qualified in the top two or three spots. This meant we would start last or next to last in every event. I remember winning at least one of the three-lap helmet dashes. More than anything else, I remember Chuck winning one feature and me coming in second. In the next feature I won and Chuck came in second.

Hardwood Door roadster midget at 16th Street Speedway.

A.J. Foyt and me at Milwaukee on "the mile" in midgets. I'm in the No. 1 car.

There were probably 40 or 45 cars that showed up on that night and many went home disappointed. Remember, Chuck and I had to start at the back of the pack and we had to pass 16 cars to make it to the front. That was a night to remember. Later, Chuck and I became great friends.

That spring and summer saw a lot of racing and it's impossible to remember all of the individual races. After getting a Champ-car ride mid-season, I was now running three different types and styles of race cars on both dirt and pavement. Everything from quarter- to one-mile tracks, including half-mile high banks like Dayton, Salem and Winchester. In midgets I finished the season third in Midwest point standings, winning three races and setting several track records. In the Midwest Sprint standings I placed seventh out of 47 drivers scoring points in that circuit. In Champ cars I finished seventeenth out of 53 drivers, getting a late start and competing in just the remaining eight races for the season. I got two fourths, one at the Hoosier 100 and another at Trenton.

My Champ car ride was the Central Excavating Special, a Kuzma chassis and it was a thrill to drive. The car was owned by Pete Salemi of Cleveland, Ohio with Andy Dunlop as the chief mechanic and "Little Joe" as the stooge. I drove 50 to 60 total races that season.

One of the joys of midget racing was when Jack and Joyce Turner, plus Anita and I, would travel together. At the race track we would try to pit close to one another and compare our thoughts on the track we were about to race on that night.

Receiving a trophy for a win at Raceway Park, Illinois (August 1957).

I'll never forget the midget race . . .

This is Bob Sowle's midget that I did so well with at Kokomo, Indiana.

we ran at Detroit one night. A local driver originally from Portland, George Amick, was driving for Bob Sowle of Avon, Indiana. He got a second place and I finished somewhere behind him in the feature race.

There was a quarter-mile dirt race the next night at Kokomo, Indiana and Amick couldn't make it. He recommended me as a replacement. I usually rode to the races with whomever I was driving for, so I jumped in with Sowle and we headed down the road. Along the way, he asked me how I was on the dirt. I reminded him that in the Northwest we didn't have too many dirt tracks so I was just so-so. When we unloaded that night and finished warm ups, I told him the car felt pretty good so don't change anything.

It ended up, I had fast time, won the dash, won my heat and won the feature, starting last in all three events.

Bob was flabbergasted.

1958 started out with a bang...

as we landed at Trenton, New Jersey for the Champ car opener. I was still driving for Central Excavating and we sat on the pole and led it most of the way. Tony Bettenhausen had second-quick time and we swapped the lead several times but I took the checkered flag first. I had won my first big race. Dueling with the great Bettenhausen for 100 miles and beating him was as exhilarating as anything I had ever done in my racing career. When we checked in at Indianapolis a month later we were leading the National point standings!

Receiving the winner's trophy at Trenton, New Jersey after my first champ car win. Andy Dunlop is standing behind the promoter, Sam Nunis.

TRENTON N.J. MARCH 1958

LEN SUTTON, shown in Victory Lane, waves to the huge crowd after winning the 100-MILE NATIONAL CHAMPIONSHIP USAC RACE at Trenton, March 30, 1958.

38

This is the reworked Kurtis/Kuzma that I couldn't make work at Indy in '58.

I ended up qualifying Jim Robbins' Kurtis for a starting spot in the 1958 Indy 500.

From Trenton, we left for Cleveland to see the car that I was to drive in the 500 with Central Excavating. It looked good in the shop. It was a Kurtis that Eddie Kuzma had reworked over the winter. It had been narrowed and other changes had been made.

From Cleveland I flew home to get my family ready for the drive east. This was April and school was still in session. Christy was in the fifth grade and Hollie had started the first grade. When we arrived in Indianapolis, besides finding a place to live, we had to get the kids back in school.

Juggling home and families was a unique experience for racers and crews. For our kids, they started and finished their school year at the Speedway school and continued where they left off when we returned to our home in Portland. We rented our house in Portland to a Portland Beaver baseball player who needed a house for the summer. It worked out well for both of us. Usually the house we rented in Speedway was large enough to share with another couple. Blackie and Helen Blackburn usually shared one with us. I remember when Pat Vidan got his job as assistant starter at Indianapolis. Pat, Marilyn and their two kids joined the Blackburns and ourselves (10 people) in a house with one bathroom. That was a pretty wild month! Somehow we made it through just fine.

Central's Indy car was a rebuild and neither I or anyone else could ever get that thing to work. If you have read Gordon White's wonderful book entitled *Offenhauser*, that car is on the cover. Andy Dunlop and his stooge, Joe, are working on the engine in that cover shot.

I finally gave up and got into another car, the Jim Robbins Special and just barely made the show. I felt badly for everyone connected with the Central car, but I was still a rookie and the most important thing to me was to make the race for the first time.

Unfortunately, on the first lap a dozen cars crashed in the third turn and I was out of the race before I had a chance to finish a single lap. I started 32nd in a field of 33 cars.

The front row had two veteran drivers eager to win and even more eager to lead the first lap. Ed Elisian and Dick Rathmann had been boasting about how they were going to control the race up front.

> "Chuck Rodee and I decided that we were not busy enough... we tried repairing chimneys."

Neither wanted to back off as they entered that third turn. It was the start of many cars being taken out of the race and one driver, Pat O'Connor, losing his life. Seven other drivers and I were finished for this 500 mile race.

Jim Robbins did not run any other Champ car races so I needed a ride for the rest of the circuit. Because I jumped out of Central's Indy car, I lost my dirt car ride as well.

In racing's often sad twists of fate, Pat O'Connor's death in that first lap opened up an opportunity for me. Chapman Root, who owned the Sumar stable of cars, offered me O'Connor's ride. I drove their cars for seven races, finishing all of them but getting only a fourth place at Atlanta as my best finish.

Standing beside two really great drivers, Jud Larson and Eddie Sachs.

Catching a little air at Williams Grove.

In the sprints I competed in eight out of 11 races, placing eighth in the final point standings. In the midgets I ran about half the races with six finishes in the top five. I also set fast time in three events and ended up twelfth in point standings at the end of the year. There were over 150 drivers competing in the midget circuit that year.

I remember one summer, when we were *not* racing four times a week, my friend Chuck Rodee and I decided we were not busy enough and that a lot of people's chimneys looked like they needed some repair. We started knocking on doors, telling people we could repair their chimneys. I believe we did about three or four before deciding we were not as good at it as we thought we were. For years after that, I couldn't help but look up at each one that we worked on to see if the chimney was still standing.

The Sumar car that I drove for Chapman Root. That's John Blough, chief mechanic, in the glasses.

Williams Grove champ cars on a half-mile dirt track. I'm leading in the No. 48, with A.J. Foyt on the outside in No. 29.

Chasing Jud Larson on the mile dirt track at DuQuoin, Illinois.

My racing idol, Tony Bettenhausen...

made 1959 a very interesting year for me. He and I were the only drivers to qualify for, and run in all 13 national championship points races that year.

Additionally, there was another non-points race at Williams Grove. I was there and qualified for it but Bettenhausen did not. So actually I was the only driver to run *every* Champ car race that year. You not only have to show up, you have to be fast enough to make the starting line up. There were names like Ward, Foyt, Sachs, Bryan, Branson and Thomson who did not make that list.

I started the year with the Wolcott team, whom I was with at Indy in 1956 as a rookie. We made the field at both Indianapolis and Daytona but failed to finish either race. This race car was an odd creation in that the engine

opposite page, left:
This is my qualifying photo for Indy in 1959. Stooge Dave Laycock stands behind me. Chief mechanic Herb Porter is on the right, Blackie Blackburn is next to him.

opposite page, lower right:
The tire is shattered and I am about to smack the wall in turn number one.

below:
Eddie Sachs and me at Terre Haute. He is probably passing me.

"As if it wasn't hard enough for my Mom, by the time the thousands of balloons were let go and 'Back Home Again in Indiana' was sung, here I was starting to well up with tears. Next, Tony Hulman would exclaim, 'Gentlemen . . . start your engines' and before you knew it the cars were coming down for the green flag all bunched together at breakneck speed with a loud scary roar. By then I was buried in my Mom's lap in big tears. This happened every year!"

–Hollie, Len's daughter

was mounted at an angle from the left front of the car and the drive line (with two universals) to the differential in the right rear. We qualified and started the Indy race from the 22nd starting position and on the 35th lap as I entered the first turn the back end felt like a dish rag. Actually the sway bar was either broken or came loose and a "zerk" fitting punctured and blew out the right rear tire. I smacked the wall pretty hard but was not injured. At Daytona we qualified eleventh, about the middle of the field at a speed of 170.713. We were still running a supercharged Offy engine and we dropped out after six laps. Herb Porter was still the chief mechanic. He was always experimenting with superchargers and they very seldom finished a

This is a shot of my Central Excavating ride, taken at the Hoosier 100 in 1957 (I finished fourth in that race). This is the same car I changed to mid-way in 1959 and won my first dirt track race at Springfield, Illinois.

race. I drove three more races for Wolcott: Trenton, Milwaukee and Langhorne, finishing only one and dropping out of the other two.

Midway through the year I returned to the Central Excavating team I had raced for earlier in '57 and '58. My first race back with them was the Williams Grove race. I got a sixth place finish and I guess that's not too bad, but my second race back with them produced a winner at Springfield, Illinois. I had now won my second National Championship race and it was on dirt.

Some of the drivers who finished behind me were Don Branson, Johnny Thomson, Eddie Sachs, A.J. Foyt, Tony Bettenhausen and Rodger Ward. I led it from about the half-way mark. Almost every one came in for fresh tires and I ran the distance on mine by staying up in the cushion, saving rubber.

The rest of the season included a trip to the 200 miler in Milwaukee where I dropped out at about the halfway mark and then on to DuQuoin where I got a fourth place finish. The next race was at Syracuse where I squeezed out an eighth place after starting seventeenth and almost missed the show. Back to the Hoosier 100 in mid-September for a fifth after starting fourth. The last race in the Midwest before coming West was Trenton where I qualified in the middle of the pack but dropped out on the eleventh lap for a last place finish.

Phoenix was next, and while it was on dirt and all the "hot dogs" were there, I qualified second quick right beside Lloyd Ruby and from the end of the first lap on I led the race. Ruby dropped out on lap nine with Don Branson now running second. I continued to lead through lap 40 but something broke and I was out of the race placing sixteenth.

Phoenix was always the last race of the season, but in '59 for some unknown reason, it was at Sacramento. I qualified fifth and ran a pretty good race but dropped out on lap 43. That finished the season and we earned a ninth-place finish for the year in point standings. I became more disillusioned with sprints and ran only three races out of 11 that were held in '59.

Midgets were still tempting and I ran 17 of the 47 races held in the Midwest that year. Out of 91 point scoring drivers, I finished ninth with three wins, one second and one third. I had quick time in qualifying twice.

While I only ran three sprint shows, one of the pluses in sprints was that after a dirt race at Terre Haute, Mari Hulman George, who owned a sprint car that Elmer George drove, generously invited all the drivers, owners and their crews out to her father's massive Hulman Ranch on the Wabash River. There were refreshments, food and many stories to tell. Daughters Christy and Hollie relished this treat after a hot and dirty race event.

right:
My family celebrating with me at Springfield, Illinois.

left:
As you can see, running on a dirt track is dirty business. That's me with second place finisher, Don Branson.

below:
In this race, I'm back with Central Excavating and taking the checkered flag for my second win on the Championship trail at Springfield. That's Johnny Thomson ahead of me, almost a lap down. He finished third.

note: Notice the added roll bars. In 1958 USAC changed the rules, requiring roll bars on all race cars.

My champ car owner, Pete Salemi, purchased a new Watson roadster for Indy and other paved tracks. I was in great equipment. Practice during the month of May at Indy was encouraging. We were posting pretty fast practice times every day. We qualified fifth and to put it in perspective, we had only the first row in front of us and could not be in much better shape.

1960 was looking good!

Chief mechanic Andy Dunlop talking to me with stooge Joe Vedda in the foreground.

S&R Special, No. 9, qualified fifth to start in the second row at Indy in 1960.

Our car was called the S & R Special as Pete had taken in a partner, Nick Rini. In the race itself we dropped out early with mechanical problems. We were awarded 30th finishing position.

Our race the following week at Milwaukee was better. We earned a third spot finish after a rather poor 19th starting position driving my Indy car. Johnny Thomson started second quick and took the lead on the first lap. Foyt was chasing him in second. It took me 50 laps to finally get into the top 10. By lap 80, I was running fifth and finally passed my idol, Bettenhausen, to take the third place finish away from him.

After that race we traveled down to Springfield, Illinois to do the 100-miler, and I got a fifth after finishing first the year before. I drove the No. 81 Central dirt car for that race.

I dropped out soon after this early pit stop.

"*Andy was an easy going, jolly person to work with. He and Joe could always make working on the race car a fun experience.*"

Here I am passing my Northwest buddy, Ernie Koch in Vollstedt's dirt machine. Tony Bettenhausen follows.

We came back in the fall for the 200-miler at Milwaukee and got a WIN! I started eleventh, and by lap 10, I was running sixth or better. I was fourth by lap 50 and pretty much stayed there until lap 180 when those in front of me either dropped out or had to pit, leaving Foyt as my last challenge. Foyt and I traded spots and I was leading it and he was running second when we took the checkered flag.

We set a record for the distance at over 100 mph average. Unheard of for a 200-mile race on a one-mile track. I had now won my third Champ car race and even the "hot dogs" felt I had a place in their inner circle. We competed in eight of the 12 races that were run that year and we finished eighth in the point standings. I was sixth or better eight times.

Having pretty much dropped the sprints, my only other races were midgets where I ran 11 races and finished ninth in the Midwest point standings. In eight of those 11 races I finished sixth or better. Not bad when you consider 112 drivers scored points. By the way, A.J. Foyt finished tenth in standings, also competing in 11 races. My hero Tony Bettenhausen finished eleventh, competing in only five races.

I have won my third National Champ race. Hurray!!

Bob Wilke of Leader Card Racers presents me with the winner's trophy.

The love of my life, Anita, giving me a winning kiss.

This is the dusty, dirty Sacramento mile. I'm in the No. 81 Central Excavating Special.

Don't try to run every race possible...

In earlier years I had driven in as many as 57 races a year. My first race of 1961 was Indianapolis and this was to be the year to concentrate on the big races. I even bypassed the opener at Trenton, New Jersey.

Luckily, this spin didn't take me out of the race, but I had to go into the pits for new tires.

Lloyd Ruby and me receiving a congratulatory handshake from a USAC official at the Milwaukee race.

I was still driving for Pete Salemi with Andy Dunlop as chief mechanic. Our car was No. 8, the same car we had the year before, and it was working well. Next on the scene was Phil Hedback of Bryant Heating and Cooling, waving sponsorship money at us. We did not really have a sponsor as such and a marriage took place right on the spot. Phil was such a joy to work with. We qualified eighth and were doing well in the race when Jack Turner got tangled up in a crash on the front stretch, bringing out the yellow. It was about pit stop time and I glanced toward my pit to see if they wanted me in for service. As I turned my head back toward the front stretch, the cars in front of me had really slowed. The brakes were not going to be enough and so I swerved to keep from rear-ending another car. I spun out but I was able to continue. We lasted another 50 or 60 laps till the clutch gave out. We were awarded nineteenth.

A week later at Milwaukee we qualified ninth and finished fourth. We came back to Milwaukee in August and got a second place finish behind Lloyd Ruby. I started eighth in that one. Lloyd was a joy to race with. He never "stuck a wheel into you" and you could run inches apart with no worry. After a couple more races with Salemi, we parted company.

"*Lloyd Ruby was as fine a gentleman as he was a race car driver.*"

By this time, Vollstedt had been campaigning a dirt car with Ernie Koch driving and I ended up in that car for most of the remaining season. Our first outing was a fourth at the Hoosier 100. We also got a fourth at Sacramento and I ended up seventh in the national standings, having driven four different Champ cars during the year. I also ended up driving four sprint races for A.J. Watson, getting three fourths and driving one midget race at the Milwaukee Mile and getting a second place finish for Ashley Wright, driving his Kurtis roadster midget. With probably 40 cars starting the race, that's not too bad.

I'm in A.J. Watson's No. 3 sprinter at the Salem half-mile. Beside me, getting ready for the start, is A.J. Foyt in the No. 1. I believe Bud Tinglestad is in the No. 10.

Hardwood Door Kurtis roadster midget before the start of an event.

Rolla's champ dirt car at Sacramento. I really liked this car. It was very responsive to all different track conditions. It was a "space tube" frame using four torsion bars for suspension. Most cars were still using a single tube frame. In later years, everybody built their dirt cars with a space tube frame.

I was presented this trophy for being the outstanding driver during the Wisconsin State Fair week, for placing second in the midget race and second in the Champ car race.

One of our popular drivers, Bill Cheesbourg, had an interesting story he told about returning to his home after an evening of racing:

a fun story . . .

There was this car that was following him with its headlights on high beam. Bill tried to pull away from the car, but it stayed right with him. Then he tried slowing down to let him go by, but that didn't work either. The car just stuck right with him with the high beams blazing and Bill was really getting peeved.

When they entered a small town, they came to a signal light that had just turned RED. The guy was still right behind him and with his headlights glaring.

Bill grabbed a crescent wrench off the floor boards of his car, jumped out, went back and tapped out both headlights, got back in his car and drove off. As he looked back, he could still see the driver sitting at the signal, dumfounded.

But let's add stocks and one sports car race

A good friend, Dave Cassidy at the USAC office, got me aside to tell me he could help me get a good stock car ride with Ray Nichels. Ray had one of the best stock car operations in USAC.

"*At Indianapolis Raceway Park, receiving the winners trophy from the promoter, Frank Dicke. Ray Nichels is on the right, behind the car.*"

My one attempt at sports car racing in Amy DuPont's Lister/Corvette at IRP in Indianapolis.

race. My car owner was Amy DuPont. I was driving a Lister/Corvette. The race was at the road course at IRP (Indianapolis). Drivers like Augie Pabst, Jack Brabham, Bruce McLaren, Roger Penske, Dan Gurney, Stirling Moss, Lloyd Ruby, Jim Hall and Rodger Ward were there and I felt out of my class.

In the first of two 100-milers, I finished fourth behind Ruby, Miles and Pabst, and in front of the former Dutch Grand Prix winner, Joakim Bonnier. But Miss Amy made it evident that was not good enough, so I tried even harder. In the second 100-mile event, after going off the course and bending the suspension, I was relieved of my duties.

He ran Pontiacs, but at the time Ford was the front runner. He had Paul Goldsmith as a regular driver and would bring in another driver when needed.

I was told it would be a steady ride if they were to run more than one car. I accepted the opportunity with glee. Paul ran all the races and I ran most. When a special race came up, Ray might hire drivers like Joe Leonard, A.J. Foyt and others, for a race at a time. I won the 100-lapper on the 5/8-mile at Indianapolis Raceway Park after getting fast time in qualifying.

I also won a 100-miler at Springfield and in '62 was the overall winner at the Riverside road course when we ran two 50-lap events. I finished third in both events and when the winners of each event failed to finish the other, that being Troy Ruttman in one and Paul Goldsmith in the other, I was declared the overall winner. The winner's trophy was about five feet tall and gorgeous, but I never received it.

During my first year with Nichels, I ran the last six of the 22 races that were run that year, winning two and finishing in the top five in four out of the six races I ran. I placed eleventh in the final point standings.

During the year I also drove in my first [and last] sports car

Owner and Chief Mechanic, Ray Nichels, is kneeling in front. Paul Goldsmith is standing next to Smokey Yunick who is wearing the black cowboy hat. I am on the far left holding the winning trophy.

This is at Springfield before the start of the 100-mile race. This is my first stock car race win for Ray Nichels on September 10, 1961.

that nobody was really passing anyone. That is until about the halfway mark and, in my rear view mirror, I noticed someone, and it wasn't Dale Earnhardt, tapping whoever was in front of him as they entered the corner. (*Apologies to all you Earnhardt fans. Dale was only eleven at that time and not driving yet.*)

As that car got moved over, he would slip into that spot and move up one position. With precision he moved up about four spots until he got to me. I gritted my teeth and said to myself, he better not try that one on me. Guess what, about two laps later he got me. For one full lap I was running second and then you know what? At the end of the front straight, I got him by tapping him *not* so lightly. I went on to win (he did NOT

One stock car race that I particularly remember was at the 5/8 mile at IRP. The track was wide. You could put cars five wide in the straights and corners. There was a sweet spot about 12 feet out from the inside apron and that was the place to run, but still with lots of room on the track to pass. I found that groove early and after setting fast time and starting on the pole, it looked like I might lead it every lap from green to checker. It was probably a dull race to watch, but I liked the fact

Here at DuQuoin, I started fifth in the No. 11 car, a '61 Pontiac. Paul Goldsmith started on the pole (No. 2) and won.

finish second) and neither he nor anyone else had a single bad word to say to me after the finish. In fact, I remember Dick Rathmann saying he was mad at himself for not doing the same thing when that driver went by him.

When the season was over in '61, Nichels prepared two 1962 Pontiac stock cars for speed and endurance runs at both Indianapolis and at Darlington, North Carolina. The drivers were made up of three from USAC and three from NASCAR.

Joe Weatherly, me, Marvin Panch, Rodger Ward, Fireball Roberts and Paul Goldsmith preparing to start the 24-hour run at Indy.

They included: Joe Weatherly, Marvin Panch, Rodger Ward, Fireball Roberts, Paul Goldsmith and myself. We were to have alternating driving chores over a 24-hour period at each track and in both cars.

We began at Indy during November. Track conditions included rain, wind and, of course, night driving. We drove, rested, slept, ate, then jumped in a different car continuously for 24 hours. Our best average for a 500-mile segment was 113.2 in the black car called the Police Interceptor, with 107.8 for the 24-hour average. The other Pontiac averaged the 24 hours at 107.3. All of us did our stint back and forth in both cars. We would each run a full tank (approximately 1-1/2 hours). Records were set for the distance and after finishing the run at Indy, we went to Darlington to do another 24-hour run. Records set at Darlington were faster and they stood the test. We ran 108.8 for the Police Interceptor and 107.3 with the other car. Remember, these were stock cars, not race cars. Also, in those days, a racing stock car was a lot closer to being "stock" than they are today.

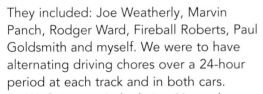

Police Interceptor taking the checkered flag at Darlington after the 24-hour record runs.

During our runs at Darlington, the NASCAR drivers who were all from that part of the country were continually talking about this "white lightning" stuff. My curiosity got the best of me and I wanted to know more. They told me it was 190 proof and while it was illegal to buy or sell, if I wanted to get some and take it home with me after the runs were over, to just tell them and they would arrange it. They "knew the right people." After the runs were completed, they took me over to this building where I was to meet someone and I would be able to get a quart of this stuff. We very shortly headed out the door and outside were two great big policemen asking me what I had in the bag. I looked around to see where my friends were and I realized I was all alone. For five minutes they grilled me as I fumbled for words and/or excuses and then I heard the giggles and then the laughter as it was all a set-up. To this day, I still have some of it left and when telling this story to someone, I offer them a chance to try it and only a few take me up on it.

I'm visiting with Paul Goldsmith during a break.

white lightning

After we finished at Darlington and were getting ready to leave, Paul Goldsmith, who flew his own Beechcraft (a four passenger), invited three people to ride along back to Hammond, Indiana, his home base. I was offered a seat which would allow me to skip on over to O'Hare and fly home to Portland. Remember this is November and while the weather was pretty nice in Darlington, up north it didn't look that good. As we headed out it was obvious we would have to climb pretty high to get over the clouds. We were at about 10,000 feet and there was barely enough oxygen for all of us. The engine acted like it was getting a little tired too. Paul, who was not instrument-rated, realized we had to get into an airport and that meant we had to drop into the clouds and find our way down to the field he was talking to on the radio (I believe it was Charleston, West Virginia). We made it down alright, but as Paul prepared to fuel up his plane and check the weather, I grabbed my helmet bag and told him I was going to check the airline schedules for a commercial flight out. I decided that bravery and daring were better spent on the race track. I grabbed an open seat on a commercial airplane and headed home!

With the Meadows Pontiac sponsor name on this car, I would say we are scheduled to drive a NASCAR race at Riverside.

During 1963, USAC allowed drivers to enter NASCAR-sanctioned races. Ray Nichels entered several cars in races at Daytona, Atlanta and Riverside. I competed at Daytona in a 100-mile qualifying race, plus the 500-mile race. My car did not finish either. At Atlanta, after dropping out midway through the race, I relieved Paul Goldsmith in the other Pontiac as he was being overcome by fumes from a broken exhaust system. After running one tankful of fuel, I came in and Paul relieved me. It took about a half-hour for me to get my senses back after my stint at the wheel.

At Riverside, the fourth NASCAR race that we ran, I was again unable to take the checkered flag and as a result, my short NASCAR career was discouraging. But running Daytona in stock cars was a lot more fun than when I ran my Indy car there.

In 1962 there were 22 stock car events. I competed in eight and had two seconds and two thirds (four "podium" finishes). We ended up seventh in point standings.

In '63 there were 16 stock car races on our scheduled and I finished eleventh in point standings. I drove in eight of them and finished in the top five in four of the races, with one second, two fourths and a fifth.

At Langhorne, one of the races where Nichels ran three cars. I'm in the Leader Card uniform with Foyt, in the baseball cap, talking to me. Goldsmith ran the Packer Pontiac.

1962 is my opportunity of a lifetime

Coming back to the pit apron after setting the one- and four-lap track records at Indy.

Over the winter, I was given the opportunity of a lifetime. Bob Wilke, owner of the famous Leader Card Racing Team, and his chief mechanic, the legendary A.J. Watson, contacted me and asked if I would be interested in joining them as teammate to Rodger Ward. This was a no-brainer!

It was the best of operations bar none.

I could hardly believe it. I would have my own chief mechanic, Chickie Hirashima, who had won the 500 in 1960 with Jim Rathmann.

Chickie was easy to work with and he got the best out of me. One thing I regret is that Johnny Boyd had been their driver the previous year and I am afraid he was upset with me for many years, evidently believing that I had taken his ride. I don't think he every truly accepted that I never went after it. They called me. I didn't call them.

Watson, Chickie and Bob Wilke are standing behind the car on my right.

Chickie's Prank

One day my speeds fell off a little. Chickie told me to go get a Coke or something while they checked the car over.

A half hour later a crew member excitedly told me "Chickie found something" and they were bringing the car back out. With excitement I grabbed my helmet and jumped in the car and found an extra 2 or 3 miles per hour.

As it turns out, I set both the one- and four-lap track records in qualifying the next day. I also found out days later "they didn't do a darned thing."

In racing, a person can be psyched very easily. Anyway, I guess I could. I broke the record that had been set by Jim Hurtubise a couple of years earlier. Within another half hour, Parnelli Jones broke my record and became the first driver to surpass the 150 mph barrier.

Probably my third pit stop. My face is black with rubber and oil.

It was the most comfortable month of May I'd ever experienced. The car was always ready and the crew was a joy to work with. We were usually one of the top three in practice speeds every day.

I ended up starting fourth with Foyt starting fifth right beside me. Knowing the race was for 500 miles, there was no way that I could win it in the first 10 or 20 laps. I tried to get a rhythm going that would keep me in the hunt. Unlike today's racers, who hardly back off, in our day the decision on getting around Indy was: should you use brakes and if so, how much? Parnelli used brakes a lot. Foyt wasn't far behind him. Right or wrong, I was taught to not use brakes at Indy. I will admit it's not the fastest, but in using brakes a lot, you would rarely go 500 miles. Also, how do you make pit stops if you run out of brakes? How do you avoid an accident if it unfolds in front of you? As it turned out, Foyt charged after Parnelli, but was out at 70 laps. Parnelli lost his brakes and had to rub the pit wall to get his car stopped for pit work on one stop, and the crew threw out tires and wheels to get him stopped on another. This was before radio communications, so information from the driver to the crew was almost impossible. Parnelli finished seventh. With my strategy, I was able to stay running in the top five throughout the race. From the 130th lap on, I was running either first or second. Between the first and second pit stop, I remember Chickie putting something on the pit board to indicate my speed had dropped off. I motioned back that I thought I could hear something wrong. He just came back with a motion, **stand on it.** I picked the pace back up and tried to forget about it. Later it proved out a dzus fastener had come loose and it was just a body panel vibrating. Also, getting ready for the third pit stop, my board indicated "next time in" and seconds later the yellow was out. Roger McCluskey had spun in the number two turn, leaving gravel and dirt up on the race track.

I was leading the race at the time

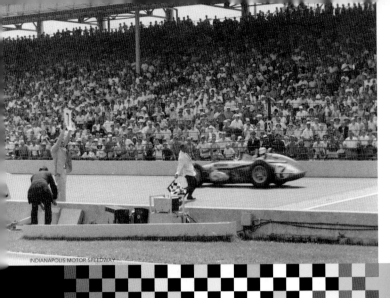

left:
Taking the checkered flag from Portland's Pat Vidan.

right:
Don "Big Red" Burden holds me up as I stand on the tire waving to the crowd.

below:
Chickie was not one to show too much emotion!

($150 per lap) and anyone really thinking would have stayed out. It just needed a couple laps to clean it up and then, with the field slowed down, I could have closed up on the field and made a later pit stop. But I came in the next time around.

Rodger, my teammate, retook the lead and I was probably 15 seconds behind after going back out, rather than the five or 10 seconds I would have been with a delayed stop. Also, I killed the engine as I started back out, but the crew was really pushing, and as I snapped the clutch, it caught and restarted. Eddie Sachs was about 10 seconds behind me and starting to push. At this point, Sachs was probably turning faster laps than either Rodger or myself.

I was getting "the board" that Sachs was closing in and Rodger was getting the board that I was closing in on him.

It ended up the closest three-car finish since the 500 began at Indy in 1911. In finishing behind Rodger – I have stated many times – I finished 11 seconds and $86,000 behind Ward. Speaking of money, last place at Indy today pays more than Rodger made when he won it! The race itself was a joy to be a part of. Rodger Ward and myself were the odds-on favorites to finish one-two.

I was given four-to-one odds by the newspaper to be the winner that year. Those were the same odds that were given to Rodger. Parnelli had five to one,

and Foyt was at seven to one. This was a credit to the teams as much as to the drivers themselves. Our one-two finish was the first time that team cars had run one-two since the Blue Crowns had done it back in the 40's.

For years after that race, people would come up to me and say, "You could have won that race, right? Wilke and Watson told you to stay put and not pass Ward, right?" The fact is, Chickie would have given me the world if I would have passed Ward and won the race. There was definitely no deal before or during the race as to our positions. The one thing I am sure of, neither one of us would have risked taking the other out trying to get to the finish line first.

Going on to Milwaukee the next weekend, things went well. I remember shaking down both cars, Ward's and my own. Rodger went to New York for some TV work and I practiced in both cars on Saturday. I got around quicker in Rodger's car than I did in my own. I remember kidding A.J., wondering why Rodger's car was faster than mine. I qualified ninth and had pretty good success moving up through the field, running fourth at 60 laps, third at 70 and second at 80. On the 84th lap, while running second to A.J. Foyt, I blew a left rear brake cylinder and backed it into the wall. Four vertebrae discs were crushed and I blew a hole in my right lung.

above:
That's fiberglass coming off the tail, not fuel. My leaning forward caused my crushed discs and punctured a lung.

right:
Our neighbors in Portland put up a welcome home sign. Note the neck brace.

below:
Here we are ready to move out for the start of the 100-miler at Milwaukee. Note the treaded tires.

Even though I got out of the race car after the crash by myself, I hurt so badly that all the way to the hospital I was begging the ambulance driver to slow down. When they rolled me down the hall in emergency, a doctor came up to me and asked "Where do you hurt?" I pointed to my right lung. He pulled out his scalpel and placed it about an inch from my nipple. Next, he said "This won't hurt" and he pierced my chest. To this day I can still recall the sound of air rushing out of that hole! Next he asked, "Doesn't that feel better?" and I answered an emphatic yes. The recuperation was painful. I must have blown up a few hundred balloons to re-expand my lungs.

After about a week to 10 days I was released and Anita and I traveled home to Portland. Anita drove the whole way while I lay flat across the back seat. I had to wear a head/neck brace for over a month.

After a couple months recovery I tried a come back. Chickie had moved over to Autolite Spark Plugs and Don Branson had my ride and was doing well. Jud Phillips had come with him to replace Chickie as Leader Card's second mechanic.

They offered me a third car and I finished the season with them. I got a second place finish at Trenton and we ended the season on the West coast at Sacramento and Phoenix. I finished tenth and ninth in those races. No more sprints and midgets, just Champ and stock cars.

> "*Everything went into slow motion and I knew I was going to hit the wall, so I held my breath. Big mistake . . . that's how I punctured my lung.*"

We are at Trenton and I am driving a third car for Leader Card. Branson and Ward are in the other two cars.

1963 brings changes at home in Portland

Vollstedt's new rear-engine car in a very early picture.

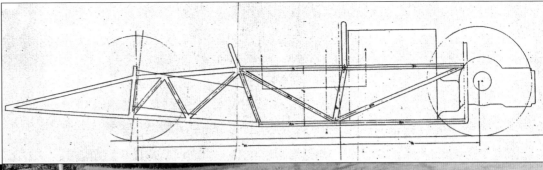

right:
One of Don Robison's original drawings.

below, right:
A side view after the basic chassis is just about finished.

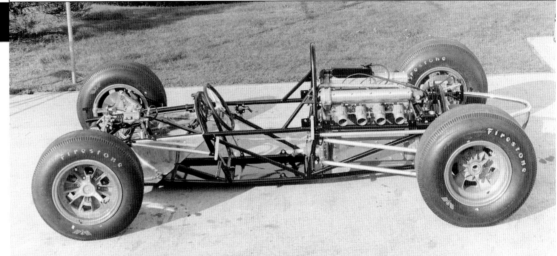

During most of the previous years, I had worked at a Ford dealership, selling cars in my off season. Beginning in '62, I came home after the season and worked for Monroe Auto Equipment Company in Marketing. That winter, while visiting Vollstedt, he secured my interest in a rear-engine adaptation for an Indy car. It looked good on paper and was already being put together in his basement.

The original idea came from Don Robison. Don has recalled how he studied books on European racing to gather some information. Don and John Feuz then looked at and measured all of the suspension details on a Lotus rear-engined race car that Monte Shelton had in his stable of cars. Monte was, and is, a very successful sports car racer who has done it all in that type of racing.

Don and John wanted to build a rear-engine car. Lacking all of the essentials to do this, they enlisted Rolla's capabilities and got started on the project. One of Don's original drawings is shown above.

In the beginning it was Don, John, and Rolla gathering information on material to purchase (basically tubing), cutting pieces to length, welding them together and away they went. Rolla was the only one spending money up to that point and he was just a working man like the rest of us.

He had a day-time job selling lumber for Jewett-Cameron Lumber Company with a pay check, again, just like the rest of us.

Building an Indianapolis race car costs money.

During the winter of 1962/63, in one of the Monroe meetings we held on a regular basis, we were in Boise, Idaho. To draw interest for good attendance we contacted a local racer, Grant King, and asked him to bring his racer to the meeting and show it off. I had met Grant

Harold Sperb

was someone I'd raced with and against in the Northwest. He came aboard to help out. Harold is probably one of the best metal men and welders I have ever known. You have to realize that it takes many hundreds of hours to construct something as complicated as a new racing car. And for the most part, it was done with free labor and at night after everyone got off work. I would say that Vollstedt had less than $15,000 invested when his race car left for Indianapolis. It would have been $50,000 if he had paid wages.

Here I am with Harold, holding the winner's trophy after he let me drive his car in that race.

before and knew of his racing craftsmanship capabilities. After the shock absorber meeting I spoke with Grant about Vollstedt's project. He knew Rolla and had raced against him in the Northwest. Grant was so intrigued by Rolla's project that he came to Portland to join in.

The car was designed to have an Offy engine, but of course, Rolla didn't even have one. Dick Martin, who owned Exhaust Specialties in Portland, stepped up to supply the funds to do that.

Thank God for Dick.

As the car came closer to completion, more funds were needed to finish the job. Tom Nehl stepped up next and helped bridge the gap to completion.

Thank God for Tom.

During the early part of the year, I had the opportunity to drive in four NASCAR races for Nichels, one of which was the Daytona 500. Although I had an engine failure at the halfway mark, I can still say I was one of the very first drivers to have competed in both the Indianapolis 500 and the Daytona 500. There were eight of us that year, the others being A.J. Foyt, Troy Ruttman, Parnelli Jones, Dan Gurney, Paul Goldsmith, Jim Hurtubise and Johnny Rutherford, who was a rookie in both events. One of the first to drop out, by the way, was Ralph Earnhardt, father of Dale.

meanwhile . . .

Spring came and Anita and I headed east. By this time, our girls were getting a little older and being taken out of school twice a year was getting old. I believe they were staying with their grandmother this time.

We started out 1963 at Trenton on April 21, and it was cold. Leader Card had three cars entered: Branson, Ward and myself. We qualified and all started somewhere in the first six rows. Mine was the only Leader Card car to finish and take the checkered flag. I started twelfth and finished seventh.

At Indianapolis I was still driving for Leader Card. I had a new car by Watson, and a new chief mechanic, Sonny Meyer. Leader Card was now a three-car operation with Don Branson teamed with Jud Phillips, plus Rodger with A.J. Watson in the lead position. This month of May was a disaster for me. I could never get the car up to speed comfortably. Once during the month I backed it into the wall in turn one (not too much damage). On the last qualifying day we did get qualified but then got bumped and that was it for Indy '63. An odd thing happened after that. I started walking down the qualifying line just to see if anything was open. I found Ray Crawford sitting on his left front tire, looking kind of grumpy. I asked if he was going out and he replied, "What for? We're not going fast enough." There was still enough time left before the six o'clock cut off to get in maybe four more qualifying attempts, so I asked Ray, "Want me to take a crack at it?" He said "Go for it." I ended up going out with about 10 minutes left of qualifying time and we made the show, bumping the slowest qualifier. The problem is, that's not the end of the story. While we're celebrating our accomplishment, Al Miller goes out

above, left:
This is not the No. 7 car with which I finished second in 1962. It's a brand new car for 1963.

above, right:
Chickie, now with Autolite, consoles me after my disappointing qualification time.

left:
The 1963 three-car lineup. Standing from the left is Bob Wilke, A.J. Watson, Sonny Meyer and Jud Phillips. Branson is in the No. 4 car, then Rodger and I'm in the No. 7.

and as he starts his qualifying attempt, the gun goes off, ending any more qualifying attempts after his. I didn't believe he'd been going fast enough to worry too much about it.

Well he did in fact go fast enough, and I was bumped for the second time in the period of about an hour. We looked at the records to see if anyone else had ever been bumped twice from the same race. We never found any.

During the first weekend of qualifying, I was emotionally wrought when my friend Jack Turner crashed on the front stretch near the start/finish line and went to the hospital with severe burns on his back. They had to take skin from his legs and his sides and graft 128 inches to his back. He remained in the Methodist Hospital for eleven weeks. Jack retired after that crash.

The threat of fire has always bothered me. After Jack's mishap I decided to rig up a fire extinguisher inside the cockpit of my race car. I believe I was the first driver to do this.

After Indy, we went to Milwaukee, as we always did and I got a sixth-place finish. This was in the Leader Card car with which I missed the show at Indy. Why it worked then but not at Indy is still a mystery. I really did not have a steady chief mechanic any more. Don Branson had taken over the number two spot with Leader Card and had the services of Jud Phillips. I was just an add on. I don't believe Leader Card ever intended to run three cars full time.

I ran one more race for Leader Card and that was the Milwaukee 200. I got a "ho hum" twelfth and that was the last race I drove for them. I finished the season in another car.

In the stock car circuit, still with Nichels, we went to Dayton, Ohio to run on the half-mile paved high banks on June 30. Nichels took two cars so that both Goldsmith and I had a car. It was a gloomy day and the possibility of a rain-out was in the air. When qualifying was over, I had fast time with a new track record. The time was 20.82 for a speed of 86.4 mph. Unfortunately the event was rained out and was never rescheduled.

At the end of the '63 racing season I headed home to sell shock absorbers for Monroe and hook up with Vollstedt to see how his rear-engine car was coming along.

INDIANAPOLIS MOTOR SPEEDWAY

left:
Ray Crawford's Elder chassis that I qualified and was bumped in, with no time left for another try at qualifying.

below:
At Langhorne we would have the back end out most of the way around the track.

Standing from the left is Grant King, Keith Randol behind at the starter, Vollstedt standing beside me and up and coming driver Billy Foster looking on.

below:
After our Goodyear tire tests and Bryant's sponsorship, the car is back in Portland. Rolla and Don Robison pose with the car.

Rolla's car was finished...

and on a wet day, we took it out to Portland Speedway to give it life. I can still remember coming in after that first ride and telling Rolla it felt like driving a Cadillac.

Goodyear was getting interested in developing a tire for Indianapolis and I was able to get their permission to come back to Indy that fall to be a part of a tire test with Vollstedt's new rear-engined creation. I believe there were four of us including A.J. Foyt.

Goodyear told us we would not be on the payroll until we hit 148 mph. We did that on about the tenth lap we ran. During that week of testing I had the fastest time (over 153). The fastest lap ever by anyone up till then, was 151.9. Rolla's car got a lot of attention to the point where Watson went ahead and built two just like it, one for Ward with a Ford V-8 and one for Branson with an Offy. Ward was to finish second with his. It was interesting that a few "railbirds" looked at Rolla's creation before it turned that first lap and scratched their heads in wonderment. When Smokey Yunick, living in Florida heard about it, he said laughing, "You better get the shovels ready to scrape that thing off the wall. When it goes into that first turn it'll never turn." I also remember his idea a year or two later, called a side car creation that did scare a couple of drivers out of their wits before being parked. That car really was a joke.

1964 started out at Phoenix...

with Vollstedt's new creation and we had problems from the start. The block was turned around to put the intake and exhaust on opposite sides. Our test at Indy had taught us that would be better. An oil passage ended up being blocked and we froze the cams. That took care of Phoenix.

This shot is in the early spring of '64 doing tire tests for Goodyear at Indy.

"Vollstedt was operating on a shoestring. Getting a sponsorship with Bryant Heating & Cooling put us back in the race"

With the income from an additional tire test at Indy between Phoenix and start of the 500 practice on May 1st, we were able to get ourselves in the black. Grant King and Harold Sperb took the race car directly from Phoenix back to Bob Sowle's place in Avon, Indiana to completely rebuild the engine. We started testing again in March for Goodyear and at this test we were the quickest at 154.9. Foyt was second quick at 154.7.

I believe Branson, Ruby and Marshman were also a part of that test. By this time, the railbirds were wishing they had gone to work on a rear-engined design. The trend had been set.

We were now firmly back at Indy and with me having contacted my old friend Phil Hedback the previous year when we were testing for Goodyear, we ended up with Bryant Heating and Cooling as our sponsor. Believe me when I say that Vollstedt was operating on a shoe string. He probably had less than $15,000 invested and there *wasn't* much more where that came from. Bryant's sponsor money was a huge boost.

On May 1st, A.J. Foyt and a couple of others who had tested with us the previous fall, donned our Goodyear tires and started our practice runs. Firestone, which had total domination of Indy racing, had not gone to sleep over the winter. Most of the other participants were on Firestone tires and it seemed the Firestones were quicker. As the month wore on, the Goodyears were being replaced by Firestones and we joined in. As it turned out everyone ended up on Firestones.

It also turned out that Vollstedt's creation (and others) began the retirement of roadsters. A third of the field that year were rear-engine creations. We definitely had the potential to make a better showing, especially after the runs we had in the fall and spring during the Goodyear tests.

Don Robison and me, with a friend of his (right) at our garage area at Indy.

INDIANAPOLIS MOTOR SPEEDWAY

above:
Phil Hedback of Bryant Heating & Cooling. He always knew how to get headlines.

above, right:
Don Robison sitting with me on the pit wall at Indy.

right:
From the left: Don Robison, Grant King, Harold Sperb, Rolla Vollstedt, Bob Sowle, Bill Devecka, Larry Griffith, Phil Hedback and John Feuz.

I have been reminded by Rolla that when we qualified, he asked me if we should "tip the can." That meant adding maybe 10 percent nitro. I remember telling him no, because the only engine we had was the one we had, and that was it. Most of the rest of the field tipped the can when qualifying.

We qualified eighth and decided that the tires would go the full distance of 500 miles. In the past, we would change tires on every pit stop (normally three) and they were worn out.

Goodyear's presence changed a lot of things. All tires could go 500 miles now. Also, for the race we used a fuel blend and went for better mileage. The mix was 80% methanol, 10% benzol and 10% gasoline. The engine would lose about 10% of its power but this meant we would stop only once at the midway point (actually lap 105) for fuel. As it turned out, because of what happened on the second lap of the race, *gasoline would never be used again at Indy.*

INDIANAPOLIS MOTOR SPEEDWAY

Coming down for the start. I am between Parnelli Jones, No. 98, and Don Branson, No. 5.

*I*n turn four, a fraction of a second before Dave MacDonald, #83, looses it on the second lap of the race. Dick Rathmann is in #23 and Eddie Sachs follows a few car lengths behind.

Getting by just as MacDonald is coming back across the track

The race started smoothly. On the second lap at the end of the back stretch, going into the third turn, Dave MacDonald went whistling by me, jumped on the binders and proceeded across the short chute in front of me. Walt Hansgen was right in front of him then and Dave drove it deep under him, but not deep enough for Walt to see him. When Hansgen came down, as that was his line, Dave had to get his nose out or turn left enough to keep from running into him.

Dave's back end got away from him and he headed for the inside guard rail. Anyone watching this unfold — *and I was* — could feel certain it was going to be tragic. By the time Dave's car was off the wall and heading back out on to the race track, I was just even with him and escaped down the front stretch. Unfortunately for Eddie Sachs, Dave's car collided with him, igniting a second ball of flame and sent a burning tire and wheel high into the air. The two drivers, from in front of me and behind me, were both killed, burned beyond help. The race was stopped for the first time since the inaugural in 1911.

inset:
I am directly across from the small white plume seen at the base of the fire ball. Rathmann, behind me, makes it through, but Sachs does not.

What goes through a driver's mind...

during that next *long* hour and a half before the race is restarted? You try to think about anything but getting burned up in a race car. I probably checked and re-checked my car just to keep busy. I needed to keep my mind on the job at hand, which was to race 500 miles. When the race was finally restarted, things went smoothly to the halfway mark. They had us running fourth at lap 100 and the attrition had just started. We made our scheduled pit stop and did nothing more than add fuel. Our tires would easily go the distance, and 14 seconds later we were back on the track. For sure, we had a finish of fourth or better. Then at lap 140 the engine just quit. A fuel pump broke off and we were through. The pump was new, but not the latest design. It was a disappointing fifteenth-place finish.

This was our only scheduled pit stop on lap 105. No tire change, just fuel.

After Indy, Vollstedt's job required he head home. John Feuz, Bob Sowle, Grant King and I headed for Milwaukee.

I honestly believe we did nothing more than put on a new fuel pump. In warm ups, the car felt pretty good and I do not remember asking for or making any changes. There were at least 30 race cars on hand and when the qualifying was over, we had fifth quick time. The race progressed well until the 51st lap when Jim Hurtubise became involved in an accident and sustained serious burns to his face and hands.

Fire had tragically overshadowed the racing season since the start of that year. It began to wear on my mind.

We finally ended up getting a second place finish behind A.J. Foyt.

Rolla had sold his dirt machine by this time, so the remaining Champ car races I drove for Walt Flynn in his Enterprise Machine Special dirt car.

> "*I still kid Rolla even today, that if he would have just stayed home we might even have won one.*"

above:
This is Walt Flynn's Enterprise Machine Special that I drove in three of the remaining dirt Champ car races.

left:
Jimmy Clark, Bud Tinglestad and myself at Indy.

pushed down that pedal after really driving it in deep. I was in the wall before I knew what happened. The right side of the car was wiped out. I was not hurt but I saw more stars and moons than I had ever seen in my life. It was probably a month later before I figured out what I had actually done, which was not take my foot off the clutch pedal when I thought I was braking.

Grant King and Bob Sowle took the car back to the garages at Indianapolis to get it rebuilt and ready for the next race. I ran the remaining dirt races for

I am waiting for the qualifying to start at the Milwaukee 200.

We did go to the 200 miler at Milwaukee in August with the rear-engine Offy and were hoping to do as well, or better, than we had in the spring. Rolla was back with us again and we drew number one to go out to qualify.

Rolla and the crew, as always, had just a couple more things to do before we went out. The chief steward came by for the second time and told us that if we didn't move out now we would lose our qualifying position. One more time by and he says, "Move it now" and, "You HAVE to take the green the first time by." This is a poor excuse, but in the rush of getting out and shifting to the top gear going down the back stretch, I believe I failed to take my foot off the clutch pedal and then

> "*I wasn't hurt, but I saw more stars and moons than I had ever seen in my life.*"

This is what the race car looked like after I crashed during qualifying. I am walking off the track on the far right.

Walt Flynn. I got a fifth, eleventh, and an eighth and waited for the Vollstedt crew to get the 66 ready for the next race.

My last race of the season was at Trenton and I was back in Vollstedt's rear engine Offy. We started fourteenth and dropped out at lap 108 of a 200 lap race. We were awarded fifteenth and the Champ car season was over.

In stock cars, after three seasons of driving Pontiacs for Nichels, we switched over to Dodge. For the stock circuit, I only ran eight of 16 races. I finished tenth in point standings with a second, third, fourth and fifth.

A.J. Foyt and me watching qualifying.

There was an interesting stock car race at the Hoosier fairgrounds.

Nichels was going to run three cars besides Paul Goldsmith and myself. Nichels put A.J. Foyt in the third car. The track ended up receiving way too much water to race on. After several hours wasted in turmoil, qualifying started with me out first. It was so wet my time was really poor. Later when A.J. went out, his car had some mechanical problem and he didn't qualify.

When qualifying was over, the promoter asked Nichels if I could be persuaded to give A.J. my car to drive. He had more fans in the grandstand than I did. Parnelli Jones had fast time and sat on the pole.

As a substituted driver, A.J. had to start last. Twenty laps into the race A.J. had to come in to get his radiator cleaned as it was full of mud. Parnelli had clear sailing with a clean radiator and lapped Foyt while he was in the pits. At this point, Parnelli was leading with Foyt about a lap and a half down. The crowd began to watch Foyt pick off the competition one by one. Watching Foyt unlap himself right by Parnelli and then go on to pick off all those spots between himself and the lead, was as exciting as any race I had ever seen. When it was all over, A.J. picked off Parnelli on about the 97th lap and of course, won it. That was quite a race.

The car being towed away after cleanup.

1965 was the start of my last year of racing.

I may not have known it then, but it must have been shaping up to that. Rolla and crew had built me a new creation and had acquired a Ford V-8 for power. It looked really good.

In the garage area at Indy with two rookie drivers from the Northwest, Jerry Grant, center, and Billy Foster, right.

On the pit apron with the car in the air, looking for the oil leak before the start of the race. Vollstedt is on his knees, Sperb is under the car; standing behind (left to right) are crew members Larry Griffith, Bill Anderson, Bob Sowle, and Dick Compton.

INDIANAPOLIS MOTOR SPEEDWAY

Bryant Heating and Cooling were our sponsors again and they provided us with the dollar backing to have everything we needed. There were 11 rookies in the field that year headed by Mario Andretti, Gordon Johncock, Al Unser Sr., Billy Foster, Jerry Grant, Mickey Rupp, Joe Leonard, Masten Gregory, George Snider, Bobby Johns and Arnie Knepper. With a line-up like that, a driver at forty years of age ought to think about doing something else.

We arrived at Indy with two cars. My previous year's number 66 was repainted and Billy Foster was at the controls. We were No. 16 and the month moved along rather smoothly. We qualified twelfth, but on race morning, almost anything that could possibly go wrong, in effect, went wrong. Before the cars are moved out onto the race track, all 33 teams have their cars out on the pit apron in front of their respective pit area. There is a 15-minute period during which crews are permitted to warm-up the engines. At a designated moment all engines fire and begin their warm up.

Within seconds, oil was running out of our No. 16 car onto the pavement. The crew shut the engine down and started an inspection. Engine panels and covers were coming off in rapid succession. Within 10 minutes, the oil line hose or coupling that was loose and leaking, was located and repaired. It took the remainder of those 15 minutes to clean up and get panels and covers back in place.

Warm ups were over and our engine was cold. Nor had the oil had a chance to warm up to an operating temperature like the other 32 starters. We finally got out on the race track in time to get pushed off with the others. I have seen

81

This is our qualifying photo. We were in twelfth position at 156.121 mph, starting the race on the outside of the fourth row.

> "Do you think Mickey Rupp might be following too close? Believe me, that's the way to do it."

Heading into turn one after getting the green flag for the start of the 1965 Indy 500.

The rear engine revolution

Colin Chapman looking up at the photographer as he prepared to go out on the track. This is 1965 and, with Jimmy Clark, they won the race handily.

films of the cars moving away at the starting line and witnessed Andy Granatelli *slipping* in the puddle of oil that dripped on the track under where my race car had sat. Andy gets back up and starts pointing to my car as it pulls away. Andy's Novi started in the row ahead of us. He was upset and he had a right to be.

At about lap 20, Lloyd Ruby and I spun coming out of the third turn where someone had lost an engine at the end of the backstretch. I had to come in for tires (flat spots) and topped off the fuel at the same time. Around lap 80, we started a series of stops. The engine was not performing well and after trying a change of spark plugs and a couple of more stops, I came in and got out of the car while they started looking at the fuel injector nozzles. That seemed to take care of the problem and I went back out. It ran reasonably well. I re-entered the race right behind Jimmy Clark and stuck with him until he took the checkered flag. He was the winner. I was down 23 laps with a twelfth place finish.

While Jack Brabham defiantly started the modern day Indianapolis "rear engine" revolution, it was Dan Gurney bringing Colin Chapman to Indianapolis which really put it over the top. Their entries in 1963, using a rather conventional Ford Fairlane small V-8 rocker arm engine proved again that a stronger engine with a light weight rear-engine chassis, could "get the job done." After starting the race in fifth and twelfth positions, they finished second and seventh. Of course, these Lotus chassis were a "take off" from their F1 race cars and their first outing at Indy proved their worth. In 1964 they came back with an updated chassis and a new Ford 4-cam engine. Clark sat on the pole, Gurney started sixth, and I started eighth. It's interesting that Bobby Marshman started next to Clark driving a Lotus that was used the year before by either Clark or Gurney and it pulled away to lead the race for over 30 laps until a low-hanging oil plug ground off, scattering oil onto the race track. The choice of Dunlop tires for that race put Clark out as their tires started chunking. With the wheels terribly out of balance, the suspension went to pieces. The point I want to make here is that Colin Chapman, the absolute leader in rear-engine design during that time, looked over our 1964 Indianapolis chassis and made this statement: "Yours looks a lot better than my first attempt did." With additional questioning about the Roadster dominance for the preceding 10 years at Indy compared to the European Formula 1 cars, his comment was, "Here the cars are designed and built by mechanics and there they are designed and built by engineers".

A DNF (Did Not Finish) at Milwaukee a week later with suspension failure, followed by a trip to the newly-paved Langhorne mile a couple of weeks after that, and I was about to drive the last race of my career.

I was starting fifteenth (not that good) but during the race things were looking better as I worked my way up to fifth. Midway through the race, a bad accident occurred and the race was stopped. Mel Kenyon was severely burned and was taken to the hospital. I can still remember Joe Leonard being one of the drivers who stopped to help Mel get out of his car. It was really burning. Eventually, the race was restarted. With about 10 laps to go, I got a muscle cramp in my neck. I could not hold my head up without help. I ended up bracing my head with my right arm and hand, and finished the race driving with just my left hand.

Two cars got by me (one was Billy Foster) and after the race, I was pretty sure I had driven my last race. I had salvaged a seventh-place finish. Vollstedt has repeated to me several times over the years that as I got out of the car, I said, "You're lucky to still have a race car in one piece." My real thoughts were focused on watching the fourth driver (Mel Kenyon) get burned in a crash during the last two years. I believed it was time for me to consider my family first and call it quits. The date was June 20, 1965 and the next race was July 18, at Trenton. I had not told anyone or even said out loud what my innermost feelings were.

Art Lamey, with Champion Spark Plugs, was talking to me about things after the race and I asked him where he was headed next. He said Chicago, and I asked, "How about a lift?" I asked if he would drop me off at O'Hare Airport and he said he would. We just talked about things that happened that day and as he dropped me off at O'Hare he said, "We'll see you at the next race."

After a moment I answered, "Well, maybe, but maybe not . . . I think I may have driven my last race."

That was the first time I had said anything like that *out loud*. I thought about it all the way home on the airplane and wasn't sure I liked the way it sounded. Was this really what I wanted to do?

opposite:
On the track at Langhorne.

below:
I am preparing to go out on the track at Langhorne. Pop Koch is getting ready to push the car out of the pit area.

We were quite the trio back then, Pop, Rolla, and myself.

George "Pop" Koch

was my chief mechanic at this, my last race. It seems ironic that the people who were with me at the beginning of my racing career should be with me for the last race of my career. When Pop was 16 years of age, he was part of the crew for my first race with Rolla and was a major contributor during our successful years of racing in the Northwest.

Hang up the helmet... QUIT

I mean, quit what had been my passion for almost 20 years?

I arrived back home as I had done many times before and Anita and I had a talk. We talked about the race that I had just driven, and what the kids had been doing. It was probably a week later when, over a cup of coffee, I said, "I think I might just hang it up." She said, "hang what up?" and I said, "Driving race cars." I believe we just stared at each other and nothing else was said.

This was the helmet I used during the last five years of my racing career. It is presently on display in the Oregon Sports Hall of Fame in Portland, Oregon.

It might have been three or four days later she sat me down and said "If you ever announce your retirement and later change your mind--you are on your own." Within seconds, I realized she meant every word she said and I guess I needed to think this over some more.

Several weeks later, I was able to reason my way through it. I realized that any doubts about *if* I should drive, meant that I couldn't really drive the way I always wanted to. The answer was there: "Hang it up."

I had a full time job waiting for me with Monroe Auto Equipment and I also represented Raybestos Manhattan, a friction material company. Both were well represented at Indianapolis.

That should be the end of the story, except that after my decision to retire, I called my friend Sid Collins, "The Voice of the 500" to ask if he would properly announce my retirement. After saying he would, he then asked me if I would be interested in standing beside him to do the radio "color" at the 500 the following year. I accepted!

If a door opens a little...might as well throw it wide open! I decided to approach Tom Carnegie, the greatest TV and track-side announcer who ever lived, about working with him during the month of May. He accepted my request, and I was granted the opportunity to work side-by-side with Tom. We did live interviews for a half-hour each evening on a local television station, WFBM.

By the time I arrived that next year, I had also added a 15-minute taped radio show that I put together, airing daily up until race day. It included interviews with drivers, crew chiefs and owners.

Tom Carnegie and me doing "Trackside." Tom was an outstanding role model as I honed my skills as a broadcaster.

At Indy doing interviews, announcements and color spots for my daily programs.

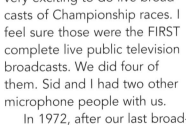

Another plus was the lasting memories of Bob and Virginia Laycock, whom I met in the early days of midget and sprint racing in the Midwest. Anita and I became very close to these wonderful people. We stayed with them each May during those years that I worked TV and radio. They are both gone now, but the memories are still very strong.

In 1970, WFBM and Sid Collins decided it would be very exciting to do live broadcasts of Championship races. I feel sure those were the FIRST complete live public television broadcasts. We did four of them. Sid and I had two other microphone people with us.

In 1972, after our last broadcast, I felt it was time to change direction again and devote all my time to my Northwest endeavors.

In 1978, with Jack Turner and our wives, we organized a special excursion back to Indy. We escorted about 20 people for a personally-guided Indy 500 mile race. It was a fun trip, but a lot of work, and we never repeated the offer.

The Laycocks celebrating their 50th wedding anniversary. From left is Virginia, myself, Anita and Bob.

2002 and I'm still here to tell about it!

right:
Rolla Vollstedt, myself, Hershel McGriff and Monte Shelton at a Sports Hall of Fame Banquet.

below:
In 1992 I drove my restored 1961 car around Indy just before the start of the race.

During those same years, our then Oregon Governor, Mark Hatfield, awarded me the Governor's Plaque as a finalist in the Banquet of Champions, Hayward Awards. Later, Governor Tom McCall appointed me to the Oregon Traffic Safety Commission for a period of nine years. In 1986 I was elected into the Oregon Sports Hall of Fame.

Our daughters, Christy and Hollie, both married and raised families. Anita and I now have four grandchildren, all grown now and into or through college. On December 8, 2001, Anita and I celebrated our 55th wedding anniversary.

Tell me how I could have done it better. And I'm still here to tell about it.

> "*I was thrilled when Len decided to quit. I still had him in one piece.*"
>
> —Anita, Len's wife

above:
At Portland International Raceway with my family, Christy, Anita and Hollie in 1984. I drove a few ceremonial laps in my '64 race car.

right:
Portrait of Anita and me taken in 1998.

An epilogue

Racing was definitely a family affair. Together we went to most of the races. All summer we would travel from race track to race track.

During an event, Mom would be nervously coaching Dad all the way. I can hear her voice as if it was yesterday, telling Dad, "Now, Len . . . ," "Watch out Len," "Be careful Len." Sometimes she would reach for my hand, needing something to hold on to as Dad was overtaking another car. I could feel the tenseness in her as she "helped" Dad maneuver through the pack.

As the years have passed, it's easy to forget the strength of emotion we all endured, as we watched Dad risk his life doing something that he loved so passionately. That was a dangerous time in racing's history. We are so thankful to have him still here with us.

— Christy, Len's daughter

My gratitude

I would be remiss if I did not take a moment to thank the one individual, besides my wife, who had more to do with my success as a racing driver than probably anyone else.

From the beginning, **Rolla Vollstedt** presented me the opportunity to be a leader and winner in almost every aspect of racing. He was always a step ahead of our competition and ready to do and spend what it took to be on top. That is not to say there were no "cobble stones" along the way. Not always the easiest person to get along with, and usually having had his own answer in mind before asking you a question, one would have trouble finding fault. The crew's favorite saying was:

"There's the right way, the wrong way and the Vollstedt way."

A while back, Rolla asked our friend and driver from the 50's, Palmer Crowell, if he had ever driven for him. Palmer's response was, "Sure I did. It was in Eugene (Oregon) many years ago." Asked how he did, Palmer said "We made a clean sweep." Rolla could hardly wait to needle me, "See, you weren't that good after all."

In writing my memoirs, you will find that Rolla has been involved in almost every chapter of my career and he can take credit as he sees fit. I also hope he will accept some of the barbs that are a part of the whole story.

Acknowledgements

This project could not have been done without the help of my family. They have shared and supported my racing career through the years. With their encouragement and assistance I took on this project and have enjoyed every minute of it.

The following people have also contributed to the process of creating this book. Their assistance has come in many difference ways.

Most of the photographs have come from my own collection, but in some cases I have asked others to share from their collections to make my story more complete.

Names and dates are stated to the best of my memory, and I have relied on friends and colleagues to help verify the accuracy of the information. I apologize if I have stated any information incorrectly.

I also hope that if I have neglected to mention someone as a contributor, that they will realize it wasn't intentional. This project started out as a small idea and grew into a major endeavor. As I came to the end of this "journey" I realized that I hadn't kept track of all the steps along the way. It's been great fun. Thank you all for your help.

Bob Ames
Bill Baxter
Gil Bellamy
Jim Blackburn
Jerry Boone
Tom Carnegie
Don Collins
Donald Davidson
Ron Parlet
John Feuz
Bob Gregg
Jack L. Greiner
Michael R. Johnson
Dick Kessinger
Jim Kessenger
Jay Koch
William LaDow
Jack Martin
Del McClure
Robert McConnell
Ray Nichels
Jerri Peterson
Julie Rawls
Don Robison
Chuck Rodee II
Wayne Smith
Bob Sowle
Harold Sperb
Christy Sutton
Jack Turner
Rolla Vollstedt
Dick Wallen
Rodger Ward
A.J. & Joyce Watson
Larry Wheat
Gordon White
Dick Wilson
Norm Zaayer

Photograph Credits

Arn-Jay: 16
Associated Press [AP]: 38, 49
Baird, Hugh: 59, 70, 79, 85
Bellamy, Gil: iv
Brodwater, Tom: 30
Bryant, Wayne: 76-77
Bushby, Ed: 11, 20
Carnegie, Tom: 87
Chapin, William: 88
Chini, Jim: 52
Clapp, Ken: 13
Coles, Ken: 77
Davidson, Donald: ii
Friedman, Dave: 50
Greiner, Jack: 8, 9
Hitze, Eddie: 39
Indianapolis Motor Speedway: i, 26, 27, 28, 29, 39, 42, 47, 58, 60, 61, 62, 63, 69, 70, 73, 74, 75 76, 80, 81, 82, 83
Johnson Photography: 53, 64
Kalwasinski, Stan: 36
Kessinger, Dick: 20
Knox, David: 41
Koch, Jay: 23, 40, 85
Krueger, Armin: 48, 49
LaDow, William: 57, 59
Masser, R.N.: 40
McClure, Del: 15
McConnell, Robert: iv
Miller, Richard: 31
National Speed Sport News: 38
Nichels, Ray: 57
Parlet, Ron: 17, 19, 20, 21
Payne, Carl: 9
Posey, John W.: 48, 64
Radbrauch, Don: 13
Ramsey, James C.: 55
Robison, Don: 71, 72, 73, 74
Scott, Bob: 32, 33, 34, 36, 40, 41, 43, 44, 45, 52, 54, 55, 56
Smith, Wayne: 46
Sperb, Harold: 68
Sterner, Gary: 30, 49, 71
Sukalac, Peter G.: 5, 6, 7, 9, 15, 67
The Oregonian: 20, 64, back cover
Thorsen, Tom: 14, 15
Vollstedt, Rolla: 7, 24, 66, 90
Wallen, Dick: 22, 25

Note from author: Most of the photographs included in this book are from my personal collection. Where possible, I have included the original source/photographer. Some photos were provided to me by friends and associates, and again, knowledge of the original source was not always available. I apologize for any omissions of appropriate credit.

Northwest [Oregon] Championships — September 1946 through season's end 1955

Roadster Championships first place   1948-1951-1952-1953-1955
Midget Championships first place   1950-1954-1955
Big Car Championships first place   1952-1955

AAA and USAC — During the years 1955 through 1965

			SEASON RACING EVENTS						SEASON STANDINGS	
		NUMBER OF RACES RUN	QUALIFIED FAST TIME	1st	2nd	3rd	4th	5th	6th	RANK (National)	TOTAL DRIVERS*
1955	National Championship:	(Races in AAA) Qualified for two. Did not finish either.									
1956	National Championship:	(Races in USAC) Entered two. Did not finish either.									
	Midgets:	2 out of 56	1	-	1	-	-	-	-	51st	110
1957	National Championship:	6 out of 13	-	-	-	-	2	-	-	17th	41
	**Sprints:	8 out of 11	-	-	-	-	1	-	3	7th/Midwest	39
	Midgets:	41 out of 65	5	3	5	5	1	4	3	4th / 3rd/Midwest	135
1958	National Championship:	10 out of 13	1	1	-	-	1	-	1	11th	38
	**Sprints:	8 out of 11	-	-	-	2	1	-	-	8th/Midwest	39
	Midgets:	21 out of 42	3	1	1	2	1	1	-	12th / 10th/Midwest	112
1959	National Championship:	13 out of 13	-	1	-	-	1	1	-	9th	50
	**Sprints:	3 out of 11	-	-	-	-	1	-	1	17th/Midwest	48
	Midgets:	17 out of 47	2	3	1	1	-	1	2	13th / 9th/Midwest	126

* Number of drivers scoring points toward season standings.
**Sprints were divided into separate Midwest and Eastern divisions until 1961.

Indianapolis 500 Records

Year	Car owner / Number	Speed Rank	Qualifying Speed	Start	Finish	Laps	Comments
1956	Wolcott / #62		passed rookie test				Accident during practice
1957	No assignment	-	-	-	-	-	
1958	Jim Robbins / #68	27	142.653	27	32	0	Accident on first lap
1959	Wolcott / #8	26	142.107	22	32	34	Hit wall on SW turn
1960	S-R Racing Enterprises / #9	7	145.443	5	30	47	Engine trouble
1961	Bryant Heating & Cooling / #8	10	145.897	8	19	110	Transmission failure
1962	Leader Card / #7	4	149.328	4	2	200	Average speed 140.167
1963	Leader Card(1) /Crawford(2)		147.372/147.670				Bumped twice
1964	Bryant Heating & Cooling / #66	9	153.813	8	15	140	Fuel pump failure
1965	Bryant Heating & Cooling / #16	13	156.121	12	12	177	Flagged

AAA and USAC (continued) — During the years 1955 through 1965

Year	Category	SEASON RACING EVENTS								SEASON STANDINGS	
		NUMBER OF RACES RUN	QUALIFIED FAST TIME	1st	2nd	3rd	4th	5th	6th	RANK (National)	TOTAL DRIVERS
1960	National Championship:	8 out of 12	-	**1**	-	1	-	1	-	8th	45
	Midgets:	11 out of 55	-	-	**1**	1	1	3	2	9th	112
1961	National Championship:	10 out of 12	-	-	**1**	-	3	-	-	7th	63
	Stocks:	6 out of 19	**1**	**2**	-	**1**	-	**1**	-	11th	40
	Sprints:	4 out of 22	-	-	-	-	3	-	-	18th	56
	Road Racing:	2 out of 7	-	-	-	-	1	-	-	22nd	32
	Midgets:	1 out of 52	-	-	**1**	-	-	-	-	23rd	112
1962	National Championship:	7 out of 13	-	-	**2**	-	-	-	-	7th	39
	Stocks:	8 out of 20	-	-	**2**	2	-	1	-	7th	50
1963	National Championship:	6 out of 12	-	-	-	-	-	-	1	20th	36
	Stocks:	8 out of 16	-	-	**1**	-	2	1	-	11th	34
	Sprints:	1 out of 22	-	-	-	-	-	-	-	38th	56
	Midgets:	1 out of 51	-	-	-	-	-	-	-	115th	138
1964	National Championship:	8 out of 13	-	-	**1**	-	-	1	-	17th	46
	Stocks:	8 out of 16	-	-	**1**	1	1	1	-	10th	37
1965	National Championship:	3 out of 18	-	-	-	-	-	-	-	35th	56

Index

Agabashian, Freddie iii
Agajanian, J.C. 8
Amick, George 37
Amick, Red 10
Andretti, Mario 81
Anderson, Bill 81
Autolite Pacemakers Club iii
Ayulo, Manuel 8
Banks, Henry iii
Beck, Wes 11, 16
Bettenhausen, Tony iii, 38, 42, 44, 47, 48
Blackburn, Blackie 9, 16, 24, 27, 39, 43
Blough, John 41
Boyd, Johnny 17, 61
Brabham, Jack 55, 83
Branson, Don 34, 42, 44, 45, 65, 69, 70, 71, 73, 75
Bryan, Jimmy 17, 24, 25, 42
Burden, Don "Big Red" 63
Carnegie, Tom 86, 87
Cassidy, Dave 54
Chapman, Colin 83
Cheesbourg, Bill 53
Clark, Jimmy 77, 83
Collins, Don 23, 25, 30
Collins, Sid iii, 29, 86
Compton, Dick 81
Cowgill, Bill 32, 33, 34
Crawford, Ray 69, 70
Crowell, Palmer 9, 90
Davidson, Donald ii
Davies, Jimmy 10
Devecka, Bill 13, 74
Dicke, Frank 54
Donker, Bob 9
Doolittle, Colonel 11
Dunlop Tires 83
Dunlop, Andy 36, 38, 39, 46, 47, 51
DuPont, Amy 55
Earnhardt, Ralph 68
Earnhardt, Dale 56
Elder, Edgar 17
Elisian, Ed 34, 39
Ferguson, Ranald 16, 18, 19, 20
Feuz, John 67, 74, 77
Firestone Tire 73
Flaherty, Pat 10, 26
Flynn, Walt 77, 79
Foster, Billy 71, 80, 81, 84
Foubert, Phil 9
Foyt, A.J. 35, 36, 41, 42, 44, 47, 48, 52, 55, 59, 62, 63, 64, 68, 71, 73, 77, 79
Francis, Ed 20
Francis, Randy 9
Freeland, Don 10
George, Elmer 33, 44

George, Mari Hulman 44
George, Tony 33
Goldsmith, Paul 55, 56, 57, 58, 59, 68, 70, 79
Goodyear Tire 71, 72, 73, 74
Granatelli, Andy 83
Grant, Jerry 80, 81
Gregg, Bob 7, 9, 30, 31
Gregory, Masten 81
Greiner, Jack 9
Griffith, Larry 74, 81
Gurney, Dan 55, 68, 83
Hall, Jim 55
Hansgen, Walt 75
Hatfield, Mark 88
Heath, Allen 9, 10
Hedback, Phil 51, 73, 74
Hirashima, Chickie 61, 62, 63, 65, 69
Hoag, Joe 11
Hoyt, Jerry 17
Hulman, Tony 26, 29, 43
Humm, Max 9
Hurtubise, Jim 61, 68, 77
Hyde, "Wild" Bill 9
Jackson, Burl 13
James, Joe 10
Janzck, Gordon 5, 12
Johncock, Gordon 81
Johns, Bobby 81
Jones, Parnelli 61, 62, 63, 68, 75, 79
Kenyon, Mel 84
Kessinger, Dick 21
King, Grant 67, 71, 73, 74, 77, 78
Knepper, Arnie 81
Koch, Ernie 9, 15, 48, 52
Koch, George "Pop" 7, 13, 23, 85
Kuzma, Eddie 39
Lamey, Art 84
Larson, Jud 40, 41
Laycock, Bob (and Virginia) 87
Laycock, Dave 43
Leonard, Joe 55, 81, 84
Linden, Andy 10
MacDonald, Dave iii, 75
Marshman, Bobby 73, 83
Martin, Dick 7, 68
Martin, Jim 9
McCall, Tom 88
McClure, Del 14, 15
McCluskey, Roger 62
McGaughy, Mel 11, 16, 17
McGowen, Frankie 7
McGrath, Jack 8, 10, 16
McGriff, Hershel 13, 88
McLaren, Bruce 55
McWithey, Jim ii, 33, 34

Meyer, Sonny 69
Miller, Minnie 30
Moore, Don 9
Moss, Stirling 55
Nehl, Tom 68
Nichels, Ray 54, 55, 56, 57, 59, 68, 70, 79
Norman, Homer 13, 16, 17
Nunis, Sam 38
O'Connor, Pat 24, 25, 40
Osborne, Howard 9
Pabst, Augie 55
Panch, Marvin 57
Penske, Roger 55
Phillips, Jud 65, 69, 70
Porter, Herb 16, 24, 27, 43
Race Tracks
  Atlanta (GA) 40, 59
  Aurora/Playland (WA) 9, 14, 15, 17
  Bay Meadows (CA) 13
  Calistoga (CA) 14, 15
  Carrell Speedway (CA) 8, 10
  Darlington (NC) 57, 58
  Dayton (OH) 70
  Daytona (FL) 42, 59
  Daytona 500 (FL) 68
  Detroit (MI) 37
  DuQuoin (IL) 41, 44, 56
  Florida 31
  Gardena (CA) 9
  Hoosier 100 (IN) 36, 44, 52, 79
  Huntington Beach (CA) 10
  Indianapolis 500 (IN) iii, iv, 26, 39, 42, 46, 50, 55, 57, 60, 68, 71, 73, 88
  IRP (IN) 54, 55
  Kokomo (IN) 37
  Langhorne (PA) iii, 70, 84, 85
  Mexican Road Race 16, 18
  Milwaukee 200 (WI) 70, 78
  Milwaukee (WI) 36, 44, 47, 48, 51, 52, 53, 64, 70, 77, 78, 84
  Phoenix (AR) 23, 44, 72
  Portland Meadows (OR) 13
  Portland Speedway (OR) 5, 8, 10, 12, 15, 24, 71
  Raceway Park (IL) 36
  Riverside (CA) 55, 59
  Sacramento (CA) 16, 17, 23, 30, 44, 49, 52
  Salem (IN) 33, 34
  Salem (OR) 9
  Saugus (CA) 31
  Springfield (IL) 44, 45, 47, 55, 56
  Syracuse (NY) 44
  Terre Haute (IN) 32, 34, 43, 44
  Trenton (NJ) iii, 36, 38, 44, 65, 79, 84
  West 16th Street (IN) 30, 35

  Williams Grove (PA) 32, 40, 41, 42, 44
Randol, Keith 71
Rathmann, Dick 10, 39, 57, 75
Reece, Jimmy 17
Ringer, Dick 21
Rini, Nick 47
Robbins, Jim 39, 40
Roberts, Fireball 57
Robison, Don 67, 71, 73, 74
Rodee, Chuck 35, 40, 41
Root, Chapman 40, 41
Ruby, Lloyd 44, 51, 55, 73, 83
Rupp, Mickey 81, 82
Russo, Paul 29
Rutherford, Johnny 68
Ruttman, Troy 10, 55, 68
Sachs, Eddie iii, 40, 42, 43, 44, 63, 75
Salemi, Pete 36, 46, 51
Scott, Bob 10
Shelton, Monte 67, 88
Sherman, Louie 16
Snider, George 81
Soukup, Jim 11
Sowle, Bob 37, 73, 74, 77, 78, 81
Sperb, Harold 14, 15, 68, 73, 74
Sutton, Anita iii, 7, 12, 29, 32, 33, 49, 64, 65, 69, 86, 87, 89
Sutton, Christy 12, 21, 32, 89
Sutton, Hollie 32, 43, 89
Sweikert, Bob 17
Templeman, Shorty 15, 29, 30
Thomson, Johnny 42, 44, 45, 47
Tinglestad, Bud 52, 77
Turner, Don 7
Turner, Jack ii, 27, 29, 36, 51, 70, 87
Unser Sr., Al 81
Vedda, Joe 46
Vidan, Pat 23, 39, 63
Vollstedt, Rolla 7, 9, 13, 14, 15, 22, 23, 24, 29, 30, 48, 52, 66, 67, 68, 70, 71, 72, 73, 74, 75, 77, 78, 79, 80, 81, 84, 85, 88, 90
Walker, Harry 11
Ward, Rodger ii, 17, 26, 42, 44, 55, 57, 63, 64, 65, 69, 71
Waters, Don 9, 10
Watson, A.J. ii, 46, 52, 61, 63, 64, 69, 71
Weatherly, Joe 57
Weedmeyer, Leroy 7, 11
Wilke, Bob 49, 61, 63, 69
Wilson, Andy 9
Wilson, Dick 21
Wolcott, Roger ii, 24, 27, 42, 44
Wright, Ashley 30, 31, 52
Youngstrom, Gordy 5, 9, 11, 28
Yunick, Smokey 55, 71
Zaayer, Norm 11